GOOD GRIEF

GOOD GRIEF

*On Loving Pets,
Here and Hereafter*

E.B. BARTELS

MARINER BOOKS
Boston   New York

HarperCollins books may be purchased for educational, business,
or sales promotional use. For information, please email the
Special Markets Department at SPsales@harpercollins.com.

FIRST EDITION

Designed by Emily Snyder

Library of Congress Cataloging-in-Publication Data has been applied for.

ISBN 978-0-358-21233-1

22 23 24 25 26   LSCC   10 9 8 7 6 5 4 3 2 1

For Richie, who gets it.

Absence makes the heart grow fonder, but it sure makes the rest of you lonely.

— CHARLES M. SCHULZ

Contents

Introduction

THE GRAVE I was looking for was in a quiet back corner of the cemetery, surrounded by trees. I was grateful for the shade—it was August in Westchester County, and the place was hot. Asphalt pathways crisscrossed rows of blinding granite headstones; my black dress clung to the sweat on my back. I'd spent the afternoon walking up and down the paths of this four-acre cemetery. Bright spots of metallic pinwheels, Mylar balloons, and neon stuffed animals decorated the headstones. Flowers wilted in the summer sun.

Under the trees, weaving through the graves, I found the marker: pink granite, engraved with hearts. CLARENCE, it read. MY ETERNAL FRIEND AND GUARDIAN ANGEL. YOU'LL ALWAYS BE A PART OF ME FOREVER. And underneath, obscured by flowers: LOVE, M.

I had read about Clarence. I knew he was a loyal friend,

kind, affectionate, sweet. Even though he ran with a famous crowd, he didn't seem to care about money or celebrity or power. He valued the simple things in life. I studied
the dates under Clarence's name: *1979–1997*. Clarence was
eighteen when he died—by most cemeteries' standards,
painfully young. But in this cemetery, in Hartsdale, New
York, eighteen is a good, long life.

I was looking at the grave of Mariah Carey's cat.

This was not my first celebrity pet memorial. I've sat
at the grave of Donald Stuart, Royal Nelson, and Laddie
Miller—Lizzie Borden's Boston terriers—their headstone
engraved with the phrase SLEEPING AWHILE. I visited Pet
Memorial Park, in Calabasas, California, where Hopalong
Cassidy's horse, Rudolph Valentino's and Humphrey Bo-
gart's dogs, Charlie Chaplin's cat, and one of the MGM lions are buried. I traveled to the outskirts of Paris to see Rin
Tin Tin's grave in the Cimetière des Chiens et Autres Ani-
maux Domestiques. I've said a prayer standing over the final resting place of America's hero racehorse Secretariat, in
Lexington, Kentucky. But every time, what impressed me
more than the celebrity pet graves was all the headstones
that surrounded them. Celebrities are not alone in burying their dead pets. To the left and right of Clarence's pink
granite tombstone were hundreds of graves for other animals belonging to regular people. These memorials were
no more or less lavish than the headstone Mariah had en-

graved for Clarence. If I hadn't known about the telltale LOVE, M on Clarence's stone, I wouldn't have been able to distinguish his grave from any of the others. *Celebrities,* I thought, studying the two hearts flanking Clarence's name. *They're just like us.*

By the time I visited Hartsdale, I'd already had a long personal history with pet cemeteries; in fact, I went to high school next to one. My school was of the New England prep variety, with facilities better than those at many colleges, on a gorgeous green campus in Dedham, a suburb southwest of Boston. This was the sort of school that carefully curated its image, boasting of athletic alumni competing in the Olympics, generations of legacy students, high SAT scores, and extremely competitive Ivy League acceptance rates. Less present in its marketing materials: that the school is located next to several thousand dead animals, buried in the Animal Rescue League of Boston's Pine Ridge Pet Cemetery. Pine Ridge was the first official pet cemetery I knew of, but there are more than seven hundred of them scattered throughout the country.

By the time I was fourteen and first saw Pine Ridge, I'd already loved and lost many companion animals. I also loved to read, and, frankly, young adult literature is full of dead pets. "I remember that awful dread as the number of pages shrank in each new animal book I read," writes Helen Macdonald in her memoir *H Is for Hawk.* "I knew what would happen. And it happened every time." What happens in *Old Yeller*? The dog dies. In *Where the Red Fern Grows*? Two dogs die. *The Red Pony*? The pony dies. *Tales of a Fourth Grade Nothing*? The turtle dies.

I could go on.

When we open our hearts to animals, death is the inevitable price. Jake Maynard, in his essay "Rattled: The Recklessness of Loving a Dog," writes that loving an animal is "mortgaging future heartbreak against a decade or so of camaraderie." Matthew Gilbert, in his memoir *Off the Leash: A Year at the Dog Park*, writes, "In the course of an average human lifetime, pots and pans and couches and lamps stay with us for longer stretches of time. Even beloved T-shirts survive the decades, the silk-screened album images and tour dates wrinkled and cracked but still holding on. With a dog, you're on a fast train to heartache."

Yet people keep getting pets. As of the writing of this, 67 percent of American households, 84.9 million homes, own "some sort of pet," according to the American Pet Products Association. And yet, despite those millions of pet owners all over the globe, and despite the inevitable loss that comes with that relationship, the ways people grieve a dead pet aren't always taken very seriously.

Imagine Mariah canceling a world tour due to "a death in the family." If her mother died, of course people would understand, without question. She would get cards and flowers; fans would send encouraging, sympathetic messages. But if Mariah put off a tour to mourn for her cat Clarence? Some fans would get it, I'm sure, but she would also certainly become the butt of thousands of jokes on social media. Fiona Apple actually did postpone her South American tour in 2012 to spend more time with her dying pit bull, Janet, publishing a handwritten note explaining her reasoning to fans on her Facebook page.* Thousands of fans wrote supportive messages — it seems on brand that Fiona Apple fans would get it — but there were also ugly comments the moderators had to delete. *Pets don't live very long. They're going to die. What were you expecting?* Taking time off from work to grieve for your pet as you would for a human — some say that's too much.

In this way, grieving pets is a disenfranchised grief, which can make it hard to know how to process and honor it; but there's freedom in that, too. With social acceptance come social standards and expectations. The human funerals I've been to run together in my mind. I grew up in an Italian Irish Catholic household in Massachusetts, so to me the death of a person meant the same open casket, the same Bible verses, the same laminated prayer cards and stiff black clothes, the same taste of funeral home Life Savers,

---

* Apple would later play percussion using Janet's bones in a song on her album *Fetch the Bolt Cutters.*

the overpowering scent of day lilies, the post-funeral deli sandwiches. Different cultures have different traditions, but every culture typically does have its own set of mourning rituals — for humans. The rituals may feel tedious and repetitive at times, but they also offer stability and closure. There is comfort in the expectedness. Even in the "spiritual not religious" memorial services I've been to, I see patterns: the same large-format photos of the deceased, the same Dylan Thomas poem, the same covers of "Make You Feel My Love."

There's no guidebook for mourning your animal. Some people keep urns with their animals' ashes on their mantels for decades; others bury their pets (sometimes illegally) in their yards. Some knit scarves out of their cats' fur; others have their dogs taxidermied. Some immediately go out and get a new puppy or kitten; others vow never to love again.

When your pet dies, it's possible you've never seen anyone else grieve for a pet. There's a good chance you won't have a model to follow. My family cremated one of our dogs and spread his ashes by a lighthouse; another I carried home from the vet wrapped in towels, and we buried her in our yard. I made a small cemetery behind my childhood home to entomb my birds and fish; we never acknowledged the inevitable death of the tortoise that went missing. For every pet that's died, the one thing they've had in common has been my feeling of not knowing what to do with my grief — I could do everything, anything, nothing. I often wished for an encyclopedia of options, a guidebook to help me figure out how best to honor my departed animal friends, to both grieve for and celebrate their lives. I want this book to be that guide.

That August day in Hartsdale, it struck me that every animal was buried there intentionally. No pet is buried in a cemetery because the law requires it; pets are buried in a cemetery because a human wanted them to be there. It doesn't matter if it is the Jindaiji Pet Cemetery, in Tokyo, or Pet Heaven Memorial Park, in Miami — worldwide, throughout history, the love is the same, and the people who honor their pets in this way understand one another. As I sat by Clarence's memorial, I watched a woman visit her pet's grave. She borrowed scissors from the cemetery office to trim back the grass around the stone. A few rows over, a man carried a bouquet of flowers. He approached the woman to borrow the scissors; she gave them to him with a nod. No judgment in the exchange, just one pet person to another. When you get it, you get it.

This book is written by someone who gets it but who wants to understand it all better. I knew I felt sad every time one of my animals left me, and I suspected I wasn't alone in this. But I couldn't help but wonder: Is mourning our pets a new thing? Why do we care so much about our pets, and why do we feel like failures when they die?

Why do we like to make and have tangible things to hold on to after a pet dies? How and why do we have ceremonies to honor our dead pets? How do we mourn for animals we've loved that don't belong to us? How do pets cope with the deaths of their fellow pets, or of their people? Who can help us with the death of a pet? Who do you turn to? And, most importantly, why do we keep on opening our hearts to animals, knowing they always die in the end? What makes this unique bond so worthwhile? What's the point of all this heartache?

Mariah Carey described Clarence as her eternal friend. She was nine when the cat came into her life, and he saw her through her rise to pop stardom. One imagines that a celebrity of Mariah's stature must always question her relationships: Who wants to be her friend because she is Internationally Acclaimed Pop Star Mariah Carey, and who just wants to hang out with good old Mimi? But for Clarence, his beloved Mariah was just the lovely human who fed and cared for him. He made the perfect friend — Mariah never had to question her cat's intentions — and his loss was palpable.

I have a mental image of Mariah researching (or having her assistant research) local pet cemeteries, deciding on Hartsdale because it was most convenient to her New York home, looking at the available plots and choosing the tree-lined back corner. On the day of Clarence's burial, I picture her in a short black dress and stilettos, maybe a black veil, big sunglasses to hide her celebrity and her tears. As the small casket is lowered into the ground, I imagine her having a flashback to some night after a sold-out show at Madison Square Garden, coming home sticky with sweat and glitter, plopping down on the couch, and having Clarence jump onto her lap. Mariah would have pet his fur; he would have calmed her down from the adrenaline rush of the concert as she quietly sang to him: *Ooh, darling, 'cause you'll always be my baby.*

Until, of course, Clarence died.

Then what?

GOOD GRIEF

Fish & Fossils

EVEN BEFORE I had pets of my own, I loved animals. A sort-of-only child, with three half siblings a decade my senior, in a mostly childless neighborhood, I spent a lot of time by myself. I sculpted dragons out of Fimo clay, worked on my novel about an elf named Norman, and practiced Irish folk songs on the violin. I read a lot of books. I had imaginary friends. I spent hours wandering in the woods surrounding my house in Lexington, Massachusetts. I never got chicken pox. And, while I grew to enjoy and cherish being alone, I still got lonely. So I turned to animals for companionship.

My first pets were classroom pets at the Montessori school I attended from preschool through third grade. There were hamsters, rabbits, parakeets, fish, two turtles named Sam and Ella (a pun that went over my head until I learned more about bacteria), a tarantula, and a pair of giant iguanas whose habitat spanned a quarter of one of the classrooms.

"Where are we sending her to school?" my mom asked my dad after seeing the iguanas. "The jungle?"

Dad shrugged. He thought the iguanas were cool. My dad has always loved animals — as a kid, he had been a regular visitor to the nature center in his New Jersey hometown, where he requested to hold and pet the tarantulas.

Mom, however, was a different story. I was born to a woman violently allergic to dust, mold, pollen, and anything with fur, feathers, or hair. She could be charmed by someone else's puppy, but only if she'd taken ten to twenty Sudafed beforehand. Whenever I would return home from playing with one of my aunt's dogs, Mom would either order me to remove my dog-haired clothes in the front hallway and sprint to my room to put on clean garments or make me stand very still with my arms in a T while she'd pat me down with long strips of Scotch tape. (Her first sticky lint roller was a game changer). I was annoyed by the process, but if this was the price I had to pay to roll around in the yard with my aunt's golden retriever, Jelly Bean, it was worth it.

Because I felt comforted around pets. I felt calmer. I didn't worry about being awkward or saying something weird like I did around other kids. Animals just accepted me as I was. With pets, I could be alone without being lonely. And so of course I wanted animals around me at all times. I became desperate to have a pet of my own. I was determined to find a way around Mom's allergies. I read every pet care book in the school library, wrote persuasive letters, casually left the D volume of our encyclopedia open on the kitchen table to the page with all the dog breeds.

But here's the thing: Mom actually wasn't resistant to getting a pet because of her allergies. There are plenty of animals out there that don't make her sneeze (fish, reptiles) — her allergies were a convenient excuse. Years later she would tell me that she stalled and evaded my pleas for an animal because she was worried about what would come next: as happy as having an alive pet would make me, she feared how sad I'd be when that pet, inevitably, died. Of course, as a kid I didn't know that, and wouldn't have understood even if I had. I just thought my mother was standing between me and the one thing that would make my life complete.

When my mother finally realized she wasn't going to dissuade me, we started small. She said I could get a fish, and within seconds, Dad and I were driving to the pet store in Burlington. One fish eventually became two, soon there were red fish and blue, and in no time at all, a very large aquarium occupied significant real estate on our kitchen counter, complete with gaudy plastic plants and hot pink gravel.

I spent hours sitting on a stool at the kitchen counter, gazing into the tank. I pressed my nose against the glass; sometimes I sat on the counter itself so I could be right next to the aquarium. Watching the fish eat and dive and dig and swim was better than any television I'd ever seen. I've since read studies that prove that watching fish swim actually lowers blood pressure and stress levels — in humans and in animals. One octopus at the New England Aquarium has her own pet fish in a mini aquarium next to her habitat. Octopuses are supremely intelligent creatures and need intellectual enrichment: puzzle boxes to unlock, glass jars to unscrew, and, apparently, fish to watch. Not so different from Little E.B.

There are also any number of stories about people suffering from depression or considering suicide finding a renewed sense of purpose and happiness when given a pet to care for. Heart attack patients who own dogs are more likely to be alive a year into recovery than those who don't; children who grow up in households with pets suffer less from allergies and asthma; dogs can even detect cancer cells through scent alone. Many therapists, too, have found that the presence of an animal in an office can help patients feel more relaxed and encourage them to open up more in sessions, especially when the patients are children.

This is why so many people are instinctively drawn

to pets—they make us feel good. So it could be that in my hypnotized state, watching my aquatic friends swirl back and forth, I was self-medicating. Being near these animals—observing their behavior and personality traits, assigning them names, writing stories about them in my head, imagining conversations with them—was more exhilarating to me than participating in a T-ball game or any other "normal" activity. "Pets give us innocent dependence, companionship, and love," writes Wallace Sife in his book *The Loss of a Pet*. "Above all, a pet is totally accepting and nonjudgmental . . . Our pets become whatever we want them to in our lives and never seem to fail us. We judge ourselves by them. Their companionship gives us added stability and purpose and a sense of personal enrichment that defies description." My fish gave me all that—that is, they did while they were alive.

But there was trouble in (fish) paradise. My parents had let me and my three older siblings each pick out a couple of fish to add to the tank, and the result was a disastrous mix of neon tetras, classic goldfish, territorial cichlids, and an aggressive betta. As much research as I'd done on proper fish care, I either had missed the chapter on species compatibility or just didn't care—I was too excited to finally have pets.

Every few days, one of the smaller fish would mysteriously disappear as the biggest fish, one of the cichlids, seemed to become larger and larger. I called him Fatso.* "Fatso keeps getting bigger," I'd observe in amazement to my parents as I checked on the tank in the morning before heading to Montessori, where my classroom pets awaited. "But I can't find that small guy again. He must be hiding." Mom and Dad exchanged looks as I went on my merry way to school.

Despite my apparent oblivion, I did have a sense that something wasn't right. A child can recognize death, even before she might have the words to articulate what's happened. According to Dr. Allan Peterkin, professor of psychiatry and family medicine at the University of Toronto, toddlers can sense stress and tension in family dynamics after a death has occurred, but they don't understand its permanence. Children between the ages of four and six, when faced with a dead pet, often imagine that the pet is still alive somewhere else and maybe, just maybe, if they wish hard enough, it will return. But according to John W. James, Russell Friedman, and Leslie Matthews, authors of the book *When Children Grieve,* once kids hit age seven, they start to grasp the permanence of death and get hung up wondering what happens to the body and soul of the pet once it has passed. Up until that point, there's a whole

---

* I had not yet learned about body positivity and fat-shaming.

lot of magical thinking and willful denial. As author Karen Russell wrote in the *New York Times* about the death of her childhood pet hermit crab: "I did not want to know what I knew."

I, too, didn't want to know what I knew: my earliest dead pets were victims of cannibalism. And so long as there was no overt evidence, I could continue on in ignorant bliss.

But then there was a floater.

The little dead goldfish drifted along the surface of the tank, mingling with flakes of uneaten food, eventually being suctioned against the aquarium tank filter. Such a small, still creature — gray eyes, wilted fins, limp thinness. I could see through the skin to the tiny organs and skeleton. I scooped his body out, and the fish lay motionless on a paper towel in my palm. There it was: cold death, staring me in the face.

I was upset, yes, but during those early pet deaths, my confusion outweighed my sorrow. The idea of forever was still hard to digest. I couldn't believe that the fish was actually, completely, 100 percent dead, even though I held his body in my hand.

Dad was in Japan, traveling for business, so Mom had to figure out how to talk to me about mortality on her own.

She hadn't even wanted these fish, her biggest fear was how I would react to their demise, and now she had to be the one to explain what happened to dead fish souls. Many experts suggest having conversations with children about pet death long before the pet actually dies so everyone's more prepared when the day comes. We did not do this. I sat on the kitchen counter next to the aquarium, cradling the dead fish in my kindergarten-sized hand, as Mom stumbled through a short speech about how fish have spirits and go to heaven just like humans do. I don't remember her exact words, but I do remember feeling like my grief was validated. Mom wasn't an animal person herself, but she understood what it was like to love and lose a friend.

According to psychologists, the most common losses in a child's life, in the sequence they are most likely to occur, are: death of a pet; death of a grandparent; major move; divorce of parents; death of a parent; death of a playmate, friend, or relative; and debilitating injury to the child or someone important in the child's life. (This is, of course, assuming the child comes from generally stable circumstances.) For me, the typical trajectory bore out, beginning with fish death at age five.

The deaths of my fish hit me hard. And flushing that first one only made it worse. There was a gentle splash as his body broke the surface of the water and drifted down, settling at the bottom of the toilet bowl. I said a few words—thanking the fish for his friendship, his service to the aquarium community. As I pressed the handle to flush, the water in the bowl swirled and flipped the dead fish. It seemed at that moment my friend had returned. I stood paralyzed. Had I miraculously revived the fish, only to send him to his death in some underground maze of pipes? As he disappeared down the drain, I breathed fast and shallow, tears soaking my face.

The flushing/reanimation trauma was acute enough that for all future fish deaths, I switched to burial. As a kindergartener, I'd joined the pet aftercare industry; with each new floater I found, I added to a cemetery that I built on the small hill by the side of our house in Lexington. I chipped away at the rocky New England dirt—sometimes for quite a while when the ground was frozen—and created a shallow hole. Then I'd wrap the fish in a piece of paper towel and place the small rolled package into the ground and refill the hole with dirt. I became such a professional at pet burial that I even assisted with animal funerals at school. Other kids' diaries contain notes about crushes, memories from summer camp; mine brags about my role in a memorial service at school for the class hamster.* I enjoyed hanging out in my pet cemetery—arranging and rearranging rocks, pulling weeds, smoothing the

---

* I got to place Cinnamon in the hole in the ground.

dirt. In a way, in their small fishy graves, my little guys were still with me.

Because I missed them. Sure, my pet fish hadn't curled up and snuggled with me on the sofa every night, but I loved them all the same, and their absence made me sad. Even after I'd gotten replacement fish, I still thought about the originals. They were part of me, in a way. I was sure that no one else had ever felt so deeply connected to their pets before, that I was alone in my sorrow. What I didn't know then: mourning pets isn't a kid thing or an adult thing, an old thing or a new thing—it's a forever thing.

"I am fascinated by how people haven't changed in five thousand years. Being so close to a particular animal, not just as a totem but as a friend and companion," Salima Ikram, distinguished professor of Egyptology at the American University in Cairo, told me over the phone. Ikram is the world expert on ancient Egyptian animal mummies. If you've read anything about animal mummies, you've seen her name. Originally from Pakistan, she has helped with the animal mummy collections at the Museo Egizio, in Turin, Italy, and the Plymouth City Museum and Art Gallery, in Plymouth, England. She has also collaborated with curators at the British Museum, in London, and the Metropolitan Museum of Art, in New York. In summary: Ikram is a global animal-mummy superstar.

When I spoke with her, Ikram told me her interest in

animal mummies began when she was a child and first visited the (as it was called then) Room of Flora and Fauna at the Egyptian Museum in Cairo. "I was absolutely riveted by it," she said. She'd always been interested in animals and had pets herself while growing up—a snake, a turtle. "I also had a hamster, but it died," Ikram added briskly. "We didn't bond very well." Even so, Ikram buried the hamster with "great pomp and splendor," wrapping the rodent up, burying her, adding a tombstone, sprinkling the grave with rose water, even laying out offerings of "that ghastly prepared hamster food."

And as it turns out, laying out offerings, creating tombstones, and burying a pet with pomp and splendor wasn't just something that Professor Ikram and I did as children—people have been doing this since at least 3000 BCE. Ancient Egyptians treasured intimate relationships with their pets; it wasn't uncommon for an entire household to go into mourning when a pet cat died, even shaving their eyebrows out of respect. Cats and dogs were the most common pets, just as they are today. Wealthier, elite families often also kept exotic animals, like baboons, hippos, antelopes, wild cows, and well-bred hunting dogs.

"Animals inhabit a liminal space metaphysically between the world of humans and the world of the divines," Ikram explained. "Animals can communicate with both worlds, and it gives them special powers. It doesn't mean you won't eat them, but it gives them a multifaceted and multilayered status in our world." Ikram put into words something I'd always felt in my gut but had never been able to articulate, something I'd sensed since I was a kid: to interact with an animal is divine.

And so, just as I wrapped my dead childhood fish in paper towels, the ancient Egyptians wrapped their dead pets in cloth, mummifying them the same way they did with human bodies. The practice of mummification stemmed from the idea that a person's spirit needed the body as a home, even after death. If the body was destroyed, the spirit would wander, aimless and lost. And the better preserved the body, the better shot the spirit had to make it into the underworld successfully. The ancient Egyptians saw the spirit as made up of three parts: the *ka,* which remained in the tomb, in the mummified body; the *ba,* which would fly out of the tomb but always return to it; and the *akh,* which had to travel to the underworld. And it seems that this belief applied to the spirits of much-loved pets as well. Lady Isetemkheb buried her pet gazelle in her own gazelle-shaped sycamore coffin. Prince Djhutmose commissioned a limestone sarcophagus and offering table for his cat, Tamyt. Abutiu, a guard dog of the pharaoh, was buried in his own tomb, with his own coffin, linen, and incense.

Over the course of three millennia, the Egyptians mummified more animals than any other group of people on earth ever have, and archaeologists have found several million more animal mummies than human ones. Mummies have been found of cats, dogs, birds, crocodiles, lizards, snakes, monkeys, cows, and hippos. But not all of those mummies were pets.

There are four types of animal mummies. The first, victual mummies, are animals intended as food for people in the afterlife. Usually these mummies didn't contain the entire animal, just the part a pharaoh would want to eat for eternity. Votive mummies are animals that carried messages to the gods on behalf of humans. The animals chosen for this service tended to resemble the gods themselves: cats for Bastet, ibises for Thoth, crocodiles for Sobek. Sacred mummies — bulls, cats, crocodiles, ibises, baboons — were thought to be reincarnations of the gods because of their distinctive markings; they were worshipped and cared for in life as if they were the gods themselves. I've seen one sacred animal mummy, a bull, at the Smithsonian National Museum of Natural History in Washington, DC. The bull was positioned as if lying down, his legs and hooves tucked under him, but he was wrapped in layers and layers of cloth, mimicking the wrapping of a sprained ankle. The strips of fabric clung tightly to his shape, and I could make out the bumps of his jowls, his ears, his horns. A black-and-white artificial eye, seemingly carved from stone, peered out at me through the glass of the display case. I swear I felt the presence of the bull staring back at me.

The fourth and final type of animal mummy is the one that Ikram calls the "most charming": the pet mummy.

I asked her how many pet mummies she'd come across in her archaeological career—just four total. She and her crew may have encountered more pets, but so many of the tombs they've uncovered had previously been ransacked and robbed, it can be hard to determine exactly what type of animal mummy they're looking at, because they are missing clues. Though if the creature has its own carved coffin and sarcophagus, and offerings of favorite foods and beloved belongings like collars and saddles, Ikram said, they usually figure that it was a pet. The artwork in tombs can help, too: if the name of the animal is written on the walls, or a drawing depicts the person and the animal together, those clues also suggest a pet. Ikram has seen a tomb painting of a cat sitting on a human's lap, batting a toy. "It's quite cute," she reassured me.

Pets often were buried alongside their humans in the same sarcophagus. Ikram hypothesizes that if pet and person snuggled together in bed at night, this was their chance to continue the practice for eternity. A man named Hapymin was discovered in his coffin with his pet dog curled up at his feet—mimicking a pose they probably spent a lot of time in during their lives. If a pet died before its person, it would be mummified and placed in the tomb, waiting for the person to join them. If a pet outlived a person, the animal usually was allowed to live out its natural life and then was mummified and added to the person's tomb later. (Some theorize that pets would be killed so they could join their person in the afterlife right away, but Ikram thinks that perhaps some pets died soon after their people from heartbreak.)

Burying people and their pets together is a practice that many pet people would like to continue today. However, the burial of animals with humans was illegal for a long time in the United States and Europe—stemming from Christian ideas that humans are the only creatures that have souls and therefore the only ones entitled to be buried in cemeteries. Some have protested, to no avail—Lord Byron wanted to be buried with his dog upon his own death, in 1824, but he was denied that wish.

There are more cemeteries now that allow all beings—human and nonhuman—to be buried on their grounds. Eric Greene, the founder and president of Green Pet-Burial Society, is an advocate for what he calls "whole family" cemeteries. He first became interested in the idea of pets and humans being buried together when he learned about a Natufian burial site in northern Israel, dating back to 10,000 BCE, in which the skeletons of a woman and a puppy were buried in the same grave, the woman's hand resting on top of the dog's head.

Ever since, Greene has been petitioning legislators in his home state of California to change their laws, and many states have already revised their rules: since September 2016 it has been legal for residents of New York State to be buried with the cremated remains of their pets in nonprofit human cemeteries, and other states are following suit. Ellen Macdonald owns the Eloise Woods Natural Burial Park, in Cedar Creek, Texas, which has a section exclusively for pets, as well as seventy-six animals buried in family plots and three pets who have already been buried in the same grave as their people. "It was clear to me from the beginning that people consider their pets part of their family," Macdonald was quoted as saying in *The Atlantic*. "For some people, pets are their *only* family . . . We share our lives together, why not our deaths?"

But while the law catches up with people's desires, a lot of pet cemeteries have jumped in to fill the void, allowing cremated human remains to be buried alongside pets: Ed Martin Jr., the owner of the Hartsdale Pet Cemetery, in Westchester, has had all of his deceased family members cremated and buried next to their animals at Hartsdale. And even when it isn't legal, people find a way.

My aunt Christine never had children. Her Rhodesian ridgeback, Clyde, was her baby. Clyde went everywhere with Christine—to holidays, birthdays, and all family events. Often Clyde had to wait outside in her truck, but he was always there. Christine loved that dog more than anything, and I still vividly remember where I was (stepping out of the library at Wellesley College into a dark, starry October night in 2009) when she called to tell me she'd had to put Clyde down.

My aunt didn't last long after that. Not even two years later, Christine died, at the age of forty-nine, from a rare and fast-moving type of cancer. Before she died, she made it clear that she wanted Clyde's ashes in the coffin with her when she was buried in a seaside cemetery in Maine. As Maine has no specific laws prohibiting humans and animals from being buried together, decisions are made at the discretion of individual cemeteries and funeral homes. But the cemetery where Christine was to be laid to rest objected. My uncle Ed, Christine's husband, was distraught and asked the director of the funeral home if there was any way around the cemetery's decision, any way to fulfill Christine's wish.

"Well," the funeral director said, "it's going to be a closed-casket service, right?"

Right.

"You can have some time alone with your wife before the funeral, and once you close the casket, we will not reopen it."

Got it.

And so Ed smuggled Clyde's ashes into Christine's casket, tucking them into the crook of my aunt's arm before she was buried.

I find comfort in the idea of being reunited with my pets in the afterlife. As a child, I was always imagining a heavenly reunion with my dead pets. My version of the afterlife was based on my dad's hippie concept of souls — that we have an energy that gets released back into the universe and joins with everyone else's to form a warm, pulsing force. I imagined bright points of light: something like comets, zooming around space together for eternity — me, my grandfather, my fish, and Cinnamon the school hamster. Even if my fish didn't look exactly like fish anymore in this extraterrestrial version of heaven, I would know their spirits were there. We would all be together again. No, I hadn't mummified my fish, but I hoped their spirits would make it to the afterlife anyway.

I had no idea then that mummification was already making a comeback. If I had wanted to seek out mummification for my pets, and if I had a little more disposable income as a young child, I could have contacted the Summum, a contemporary religious group in Utah that practices modern mummification of humans and pets. The religion was founded in 1975 by Claude Nowell, later known as Corky Ra, who claimed he'd been visited by "advanced beings who revealed to him the nature of creation." Nowell began to share the knowledge these beings had imparted to him, and in 1977, he and a group of followers built a pyramid in Salt Lake City. This pyramid is where the Summum gather, teach, and practice a modern version of mummification. Corky Ra, upon his death in 2008, was mummified himself, making him officially the first person to undergo modern mummification treatment. The Summum believe that "death does not snuff out a person's awareness or ability to feel. Though bereft of a body, our consciousness, or essence, sticks around—and gets thoroughly confused by the change in circumstances." Preserving the body through mummification gives our consciousness a space to rest— not all that different from the ancient Egyptian idea that the body is the spirit's house.

The Summum's practice is not restricted to humans. Su Menu, president of Summum, had her poodle, Maggie, sealed in a beautiful, lifelike bronze "mummiform" (what the Summum call a sarcophagus)—designed and engraved to look just like Maggie had in real life, down to the way her fur curled. I learned about Maggie and Menu through Amy Finkel's incredible documentary *Furever*. Finkel was welcomed into the Summum's orange pyramid in Salt Lake City, where she filmed Summum counselors

Ron Temu and Bernie Aua mummifying a cat. In the documentary, Menu explained that she wants to be mummified one day and that she wanted that same care and attention given to Maggie in her death. Watching the footage of Temu and Aua carefully washing the deceased cat, smoothing the fur with the preservation gel, and then wrapping her in long white bandages, I could see the appeal of the process. There was a reverence in their motions and a love, even if this cat was not their cat.

The Summum no longer take interview requests, but Aua put me in touch with a man named Vern, who'd had his dog mummified in 2018.

When I asked Vern over the phone what his dog's name was, I wasn't sure I heard him correctly over the noise in the café surrounding me. I asked him to spell it. "Just like it sounds," he said. "*S-i-l-l-y, N-u-g-g-e-t.*" Silly Nugget. She was a basenji, and she'd lived for eighteen years, four and a half months. When Vern and I spoke in March 2019, Silly Nugget (or simply "Silly") had been dead one year, almost to the day. Vern explained that, technically, Silly was his brother's dog, and it had been his brother's idea to pursue mummification when she died; he was inspired by her breed's history. The basenji originated in Africa many millennia ago. Paleontologists have found that the first domesticated dogs looked an awful lot like basenjis, and that the earliest members of the breed were brought up from the interior of Africa on the Nile as presents to the pharaohs. When archaeologists find mummified dogs in Egypt, they're usually basenjis. Vern told me that his brother felt it was right for Silly to be mummified, just as her ancestors had been. "It was also a way for her to be with us, and not fully gone," Vern said. His brother did the research, and Vern dealt with the logistics. All in all, it took about seven months for Silly Nugget to transform into a mummy. The process takes a while, but also, apparently, the Summum had gotten a little bogged down with back orders. It seems a lot of people want to have their pets mummified. I don't know exactly how many pet mummies the Summum make each year, but I know that in 2005, according to an interview Corky Ra did with CBS News, more than fourteen hundred people had already signed up to be mummified upon their deaths. My guess is that the Summum have made more pet mummies than they have human ones—both because of the lower price point and because there are fewer taboos surrounding a dead animal's body than a dead human's. There are so many religious, cultural, and societal concerns that might keep the family of a deceased person from following through with their loved one's desire to become a mummy, but no one is stopping you if that's what you want to do with your pet.

The Summum follow a process not dissimilar from the ancient Egyptians'. First the body is gently bathed on the outside, then the internal organs are removed via incision, washed, and returned to the body. Next the whole body is soaked in a preservation liquid (the exact recipe of which is a secret known only to the Summum), then wrapped in cotton gauze, encased in polyurethane, and covered in fiberglass and resin. The final step involves placing the mummified body into the sarcophagus and pumping the chamber full of the inert gas argon, to help prevent the body from decomposing. And, if you want, Aua will send you photos throughout the process so you can be reassured that the Summum aren't pulling a fast one.

Which is good, because it isn't cheap to get your pet mummified; the group charges anywhere from $4,000 to $28,000 to mummify a pet, depending on the animal's weight. (The low end of that range is reserved for cats and dogs under fifteen pounds.) Plus, a customized "mummi-form"—like the one Menu did for her poodle—will run you an additional $5,000 to $100,000.

"So, after everything, she's whole in there?" I asked Vern.

"Preserved and whole," Vern confirmed. It was impor-tant to Vern and his brother that Silly remain intact in death; I mentioned taxidermy as another preservation op-tion, and Vern was quick to tell me his thoughts. "Taxi-dermy is horrible, brutal, it's cruel—they just take off the skin and put it over Styrofoam. How can that contain the essence of what you just loved?"

I asked Vern how he felt when Silly was returned to him. Even though she hadn't been dismantled and stuck to a foam form, was it still upsetting? Confusing? Did the mummy contain his dog's essence? "It was heartwarming," he said emphatically. The mummiform is a bit bigger than the basenji was in life, as Silly had to fit inside the mold, but her mummified self sits right next to Vern's brother's chair, in a shape similar to how she would lie down to sleep when she was alive. Inside the mummiform, along with her mummified body, are two of her favorite toys, including the torn-up leg of a stuffed moose. After describing Silly's final resting place, Vern paused and said, "Her presence can be felt." Menu said much the same thing about her poodle, Maggie, in *Furever:* "Her body may have passed on, but her essence is still here."

What I found most compelling, though, was how both Vern and Menu described the process — gathering photos to help design the mummiform, seeing the images of the mummification in process, the many months it took for everything to come together. Grief is a process, and one that can't be rushed. Having tasks that you can do as you cry, as you reflect, as you remember the animal you loved — and still love — gives direction and focus. Planning a wake, writing an obituary, organizing a burial, figuring out how to ship your dog's body to Salt Lake City — they serve a purpose. I don't doubt that Vern and Menu can feel the essence of Silly Nugget and Maggie when they are near their mummified forms. I remember sitting by the small graves of my fish, on the small hill by my house, and feeling certain I could see their little ghosts swimming in front of me. But perhaps part of that feeling comes only after you've taken the time to let yourself be sad, to dig deep and remember.

Two and a half decades after my first fish death, I took a job as a nanny to a five-year-old girl who lived down the street from me in Cambridge — the sort of job one gets after finishing a graduate degree in the arts. A few months into nannying, I picked the girl up from school one Monday and she told me that over the weekend she'd gotten fish.

"Oh, yeah?" I said enthusiastically. New pets, even if not my own, still stir up that same old excitement in me.

"But they're all dead now," she said, casually sipping her juice box. "The filter didn't work right. Want to see where I buried them?"

When we got to her home, my charge directed me to a tree by the front door. She pointed to a small pile of fresh dirt, neatly packed into the ground. She clambered over and patted the dirt down. She paused for a minute, studying the little mound. Could she see their ghosts swimming in front of her? Did she feel their essence?

"They're in there," she said. "Bye, fish."

Watching her pat down the dirt on the little fish grave was like going back in time. Once again, I was on the hill by the side of my house, chipping away at frozen dirt, rolling up a limp, dead little fish in a paper towel. Twenty-five years later, kids were doing the same thing. Of course they were: mourning pets is nothing new.

Birds & Bonding

$\mathcal{M}$OM SHOULD have known. The fish were nice, but they weren't enough.

I did love my fish, but I wanted a pet that was interactive. I wanted a pet that I could touch or, at the very least, make eye contact with. I got in the habit of reading the classified ads in the *Boston Globe,* looking for people giving away canary chicks or selling an exotic reptile. I would clip out these ads and leave them around the house. I wrote pathetic letters and left them on my mom's bedside table. I brought up animals whenever I could. My mom was still hesitant about the trauma that would come when a larger, more animated, warmer and fuzzier pet died. She'd seen how hard I'd taken the fish. Eventually, though, she caved.

"What finally wore you down?" I asked my mom, years later, as an adult.

"You wouldn't shut up."

In the summer of 1992, Mom said that I could get a bird. I'll never forget when we went to the small pet store in Belmont, packed full of sacks of dog food, bags of bones, boxes of squeaky toys, birdcages, and fish tanks stacked to the ceiling. Picking out the bird itself was a blur — I somehow ended up with a Gloster consort canary; I think my grandmother was involved in the decision — but what I remember most is sitting in the car on the way home, holding the cardboard box, feeling the presence of a living creature hopping around inside.

I named him Kiki, and I adored him. He was plump and fluffy, his gold and brown feathers glistening, a small tagging bracelet around his ankle. He loved to eat florets off hunks of broccoli, play on his white plastic swing, and ding the little bell hanging from the ceiling of his cage. I spent hours sitting on a kitchen stool, peering into his cage. In the end, he wasn't much more interactive than the fish, but he still felt like a step up. Just being near this bird, watching him fluff his feathers and hop around his cage, was transcendent. He was responsive, animated, and I was sure we were best friends.

I'd like to pause for a minute here to point out that I was far from the only only child (or sort-of-only child) to feel this way about her pets. My college friend Shelly, who grew up an only child, had a cat named Panda. Shelly's birthday is January 27, and Panda's birthday was January 28, and for years, Shelly would host a joint birthday party for her and her cat. Shelly's best (human) friend, Nicole, would write birthday cards from the perspective of her cat, Pointer, to Panda. "Only children have intense connections with their pets," Shelly agreed. "At home, it's just you and your parents. So the closest thing to your level is a pet." Panda lived for seventeen years, from the time Shelly was seven until she was twenty-four, and even after the cat died, when Shelly was at law school, she lived on in family lore as Shelly's sibling. Her own kids even refer to the cat using the Punjabi word for *aunt:* Panda Masi. Raised Hindu, Shelly sometimes considers the reincarnation possibilities for Panda — her dad is convinced that Panda is now a regal Bengal tiger living in the jungle of India. Shelly, though, sees some of Panda in her daughter. "My daughter is mischievous and sassy, and Panda was very sassy, but then again my mother and I are also quite sassy. Punjabi women in general are sassy," Shelly reflected. "Panda fit right in with the sassy Punjabi women brigade of Stockbridge, Georgia."

Another only child, a friend of a friend named Shweta, who grew up in Oman and India, had a dog named Dolly. Dolly was a Finnish spitz, and she had white socks on her paws, "but the socks looked like they were unraveling," Shweta said. When her parents brought Dolly home, Shweta was "ecstatic to have a sibling." And that was how Shweta was introduced to the dog: her father pointed at

Shweta and told Dolly that Shweta was her *chechi*—"elder sister" in Malayalam. Dolly really was raised like one of the family: she ate the same food that Shweta and her parents did, slept inside, lounged on furniture. This was all especially unusual for India in the late 1980s and early 1990s, when very few people had dogs, and if they did, they lived outside as guard dogs. "She lived with us as one of us," Shweta said. Dolly, just like Panda, lived for seventeen years, from when Shweta was seven until she was twenty-four, and her spirit lives on. Shweta's dad now writes letters in Dolly's voice to Shweta's children—a ghost dog narrating the family's activities. "Every day there is an email waiting from Dad as Dolly with a photo of her, and he always signs the messages 'A lot of hugs, licks, and kisses for your noses.'" When I asked Shweta if she thought her bond with Dolly was particularly close because she was an only child, she instantly agreed: "Most of my close friends are only children, most had really important pets in their lives. Dolly was a different kind of sister."

And if your pet is your sister or brother, then it should be no surprise, really, that you want to treat them just as your family treats you. The pet store had informed me that Kiki's birthday was in July, so the following summer I threw the bird an elaborate birthday party while my family was renting a house on Fishers Island, a small island off the coast of Connecticut. (Because of course Kiki came with us on vacation, his birdcage rattling and the little bell dinging in the back of my mom's station wagon for the whole two-hour car ride and forty-five-minute ferry trip.) I made party hats out of construction paper for my stuffed animals. I borrowed plates and silverware from the kitchen and insisted on making a cake from a box of mix. I cut up homemade confetti, used my allowance to buy streamers from the grocery store, and invited everyone I knew: my parents, my teenage siblings, my stuffed animals, and my imaginary friends. This was what you did to show a friend you cared about them. I had observed how my parents threw me elaborate birthday parties—with balloons and party hats, cakes with floral icing, and piles of presents. This was what love looked like.

Because I loved that bird. Sure, maybe I wasn't always the most responsible about his care. Mom would be quick to point out here that she was the one who regularly scraped the bird poop off the kitchen counter.* She was the one who remembered to buy broccoli and wax paper to line the bottom of his enclosure. Dad was the one who cut Kiki's nails—a process so stressful I often couldn't even watch it.

---

* Kiki had a charming and unique habit of hopping up from his perch and hanging on to the side of the cage while defecating, splattering little bits of bird feces everywhere except on the wax paper lining the bottom of his cage.

In the summer of 1994, my parents and I spent six weeks in France for Dad's job, a trip too far for Kiki to take, so even my poor grandparents got stuck caring for him.

But I felt a connection to him as I had to no other animal before. Sure, he was scared to leave his cage, and no, he didn't snuggle with me in bed at night, but he was another living being who responded to me, who noticed me, who perked up when I brought him a fresh stick of birdseed. And the years went by — 1992 all the way through 1996 — and Kiki remained. I even persuaded my family to let me get a second bird, a zebra finch named Finy, as a companion for Kiki. I loved that damn bird. So much.

And then came July 10, 1997, a date I would record in my diary with somber formality. I was nine years old, and I returned from my classical violin day camp that summer afternoon and found Kiki on the bottom of his cage, unresponsive to food or touch. My friend. Not moving. My very best friend. Still. My breaths came fast and shallow, and Mom, trying to decide on the best course of action, flipped through the Yellow Pages to find a vet in the area that treated birds. The option that made the most sense was in Littleton, which was, at that time of day, forty minutes northwest of our house in Lexington. "What were we thinking?" my mom reflected years later. "I drove all the way to Littleton for a bird? A bird that was already clearly dead?" But Mom knew how much I cared about Kiki. She saw how I loved him, and she loved me, so she braved rush hour traffic to take her daughter and her daughter's dead bird to a small veterinarian office in an even smaller town. When we got to the Littleton office, the vet — gently, kindly — confirmed that Kiki was indeed dead, and in a flurry of hot tears, I ran outside and leaned on the back of my mom's station wagon, inconsolable.

Mom and I brought Kiki's body back home, and I buried him in a shoebox on the hill in our yard, next to the fish graves. After that, I channeled my pet energies into taking care of Finy, the remaining zebra finch; I even convinced Mom to let me get a second zebra finch to keep Finy company.* But Finy and Other Zebra Finch died in quick succession after Kiki, perhaps all of them succumbing to the same bird flu. ("For a while it seemed like every time we came home there was another dead bird," Mom says of that period.) I was sad about the zebra finches' deaths as well, and I buried them in the pet cemetery, too, though their deaths didn't hit me as hard as Kiki's.

My mom was right. Damn. But should I have listened to her? Should I never have opened up to a pet, protected my heart from that inevitable sorrow? To paraphrase Milan Kundera in *The Unbearable Lightness of Being,* love for pets is voluntary. No one forgets to take a birth control pill

---

* The second finch's name has been lost to the sands of time.

one morning and ends up with a kitten nine months later. Pets are a choice. But they are a choice that people make again and again, to the point that getting a pet is one of the first things people do with a little bit of disposable income. "Dog ownership, like cocaine use, can be seen as an economic indicator," wrote Theresa Bradley and Ritchie King for *The Atlantic*. At the time of their article in 2012, India had one of the lowest rates of pet dogs in the world — only four dogs for every thousand people — but one way of illustrating the country's steep economic rise is to look at how that figure has changed with time: the number of pet dogs in the country grew by 58 percent from 2007 to 2012. A grad school friend, Abbigail, who grew up in Vietnam, didn't really get the whole pet thing when she first moved to the United States. Back in Vietnam, if people had dogs and cats, they lived outside and didn't last long. Abbigail said that people had bigger things to worry about: "When the level of life is not great for human beings, there is just no energy to worry about what happens to animals." Now, though, Abbigail said she sees more and more people with designer breeds in Vietnam, letting their animals live inside. It seems as soon as people have any cash to spare, it goes to pets.

People are willing to and want to spend money on their pets. Pet products and pet care make up a multi-billion-dollar industry; according to the American Pet Products

Association, Americans spent $103.6 billion on their animals in 2020. In recent years, Americans have spent close to half a billion dollars on pet Halloween costumes alone.

In particular, people seem especially willing to pay whatever it takes to help their pets live healthier, longer lives. There are whole companies out there now, like Animal Biosciences, in Boston, devoted to improving the "health span" of our pets—not necessarily getting pets to live longer, but making sure the years they do have are healthier and happier—because at the end of the day, no matter how much money you spend on your pet, they're always going to die eventually.

Why do we keep doing this to ourselves? It makes sense that little kids who haven't experienced death get duped into falling in love with pets—they don't know what to expect. And yet, very few pet people I've spoken with have written off pets, citing a loss that was too hard to go through again. Some people take longer to recover than others, but most pet people I know do, eventually, rebound. So how come, again and again, we put ourselves through such anguish? As Nicole Chung wrote in an essay for *Time* about her family's decision to get a pandemic puppy, in the wake of intense grief: "Sometimes, because I've lost two parents in two years, I'm afraid to love another being that's mortal. But even when we're in the deepest pain, we need to love and be loved." Or, as the writer Julian Barnes once put it, in a letter to fellow writer Zadie Smith: "It hurts just as much as it is worth."

I think back to Clueless Little E.B., who stubbornly ignored her mom's concerns and insisted on a pet, despite the consequences. She may have been naive about death, but she was wise about something else: we can be our most private and personal versions of ourselves around our pets. I grew up without a lot of other kids my age. No neighborhood gang, no crew of cousins, only a small group of Montessori classmates. I panicked around my peers. I always felt like the jokes I made didn't land, or I would bring up some book no one else had read, or I'd say I didn't feel like playing kickball and get a weird look. Being around my birds and fish — I could put on a bad Australian accent or belt out lyrics from *Jesus Christ Superstar.* I could be my most pure self.

In a way it was selfish: my pets were my captive audience. They had no choice but to be there for me. Pets bolster your emotional state; you grab them and hug them and kiss them, and maybe they claw at you or squirm away, but a lot of them just suffer through it. That taco costume you put on your tortoise? He doesn't know it's Halloween, he doesn't care, he can't even consent to wearing it — that's all for you. Your dog is not invested in learning every Andrew Lloyd Webber soundtrack — you're singing for yourself, really. But having pets around is a way to have an audience, to feel companionship, completely without judgment.

And with Kiki there were moments of genuine connection, too. He would flutter his wings, shuddering with anticipation, when I put a new seed stick into his cage. Sometimes he would trill some notes back as I sang him show tunes. The bird accepted me, provided companionship, and quelled my anxiety. The ritual of caring for him, of coming home and sitting on the stool by the kitchen counter watching him, was like a cleansing wash, a meditation, that let the rest of the day fall away. Kiki also taught me how to be myself—or that it was okay to be myself; he liked my being there, no matter what. I definitely learned how to care for and love other creatures through Kiki, but Kiki taught me to love myself, too.

"Animals don't exist in order to teach us things," wrote Helen Macdonald in her essay "What Animals Taught Me About Being Human," in the *New York Times*, "but that is what they have always done, and most of what they teach us is what we think we know about ourselves . . . We use animals as ideas to amplify and enlarge aspects of ourselves, turning them into simple, safe harbors for things we feel and often cannot express." We learn powerful messages through our friendships with our pets. Sy Montgomery wrote a whole book about the life lessons she's learned from her encounters with animals, *How to Be a Good Crea-*

ture. The bonds that so many of us feel with our pets are those of friendship—but animals can also be powerful mentors. "I can tell you that teachers are all around to help you: with four legs or two or even eight; some with internal skeletons, some without," writes Montgomery in her memoir. "All you have to do is recognize them as teachers and be ready to hear their truths."

And for children, that is especially true. Children learn a lot from their pets. As psychologist Elizabeth Anderson puts it in her book *The Powerful Bond Between People and Pets,* "Nothing less than alchemy is involved when animals and children get together, and the resulting magic has healing properties." Indeed, Hal Herzog, legendary animal behaviorist, writes about studies showing that "growing up with pets is linked to higher self-esteem, cognitive development, and social skills." Though, of course, in order to have pets in the first place, kids probably already have access to other socioeconomic benefits, which help, too.

Anecdotally, as I researched this book I found that most of the people who wanted to talk to me about their many and beloved childhood pets were white and from upper- and middle-class families, often from the suburbs. The people who have disposable income to spend on pets, of course, have disposable income to spend on other things, too. I understand that the many experiences I have had with pets aren't available to everyone—from the thousands of dollars my parents spent on my personal pets to the nature-filled vacations I took with my family with Kiki in tow to the fact that I went to schools with the means to have elaborate classroom zoo setups. (I can't even imagine the electric bill just to heat the giant iguana enclosure at Montessori.) But when these experiences are available to children—and I wish they were available to all children everywhere—they show just how much kids benefit from interactions with animals. Kids learn kindness and compassion from taking care of pets. They have to imagine what it's like to be someone else, to be gentle, give space and distance, read body language, feed and water and provide health care. The qualities we learn from caring for our pets make us better people. "You cannot care for a pet if you only care for yourself," writes Meg Daley Olmert in her book about the human-animal bond, *Made for Each Other.* She describes pets as "an antidote to narcissism," noting that when people have animals in their lives they feel more generous, act less selfish, and are often generally more approachable, which improves not just their health but the health of their community. When people learn to care about pets, they can learn how to care for other beings outside of themselves, and that in turn can make them more empathetic, more generous, more kind to their fellow humans.

Animals open us up to the unexpected. My friend

Mariel was absolutely petrified of dogs growing up. Mariel and I met in high school—the one next to the pet cemetery—where she often felt different and out of place. She was an immigrant, born in the Dominican Republic, and commuted to the school from Boston, unlike the wealthy white kids from the suburbs who made up the majority of the student body. Wealthy white suburban kids who always had dogs. Up until Mariel was in her twenties, she would jump up on a couch if she saw a dog inside the house, even a small, scrawny dog, and she found that her new classmates and their parents were horrified when she politely asked if their dogs could stay out of the room when she was over. "That was one of the first things that made me feel unwelcome and different at school," Mariel said. In the DR, Mariel grew up understanding that dogs guard the house. They don't come indoors; they're either strays or chained up outside, and they all have fleas or rabies or both. Mariel said she had heard about cute small house dogs that rich kids in the DR had, but she'd never seen one herself. Her own personal experience with dogs was much different: "I've been chased around the hood by a freakin' angry dog!" Mariel laughed on the phone. Which brings us to A.J., a little Pomeranian that belonged to Mariel's aunt and "bruncle" (her mother's younger brother, only two years older than Mariel, thus brother-uncle). *Great*, Mariel thought when she heard about A.J. *Another house with a dog I have to avoid.* But A.J. was always at Mariel's aunt's place, so she couldn't really avoid him.

"I would hear the jingling of his necklace or whatever — his collar? Is that what it's called? — and have a physiological reaction," Mariel said. "Just immediately afraid." But miraculously, A.J. seemed to know this, and treated Mariel with care. Whenever he approached her, A.J. would put his head down and stay very still; he barked at everyone else but not Mariel. And Mariel eventually, tentatively, began to reach out and pet him.

Through the following years, Mariel and A.J. bonded. When she was in grad school, the day finally came when her aunt called to tell her that A.J. had died, and she went running out of her Harvard classroom, tears running down her face. "I was shattered," she said. "I had never had a pet before. I couldn't understand what was happening to me. I thought, *Oh my God, I've become like these white people.*" Mariel sat on a bench in Harvard Square and bawled, eventually texting a couple of friends about what had happened. They responded with their own stories of their dogs' deaths, and Mariel felt a wave of relief — she wasn't alone. She had surprised herself with the depth of emotion she felt for A.J. He had helped her get over her fear of dogs and tricked her into falling in love with him in the process.

Our connection to animals is essential for all of the reasons above, but for some people it goes well beyond that.

Some people are specifically matched with specially trained dogs that are indispensable to those people's survival. There are diabetic and epileptic people who partner with animals that can detect an oncoming seizure or a blood sugar low, paraplegic people who work with animals that can open doors and fetch objects. There are even animals that are trained to show someone in the throes of a psychotic episode what is real and what is a hallucination. These animals and humans work together as a team, and they rely on each other for survival. The bond that's made there is unlike any other.

Kate Katulak was born with sight but lost it suddenly after an illness in high school. "My whole world was changed," Kate told me. Now she had to learn how to move through the world and find her way as she never had before, all with a long white cane. She also, understandably, experienced a lot of anxiety. As she weighed her options for support, Kate was drawn to the idea of a guide dog. She's loved animals since she was a child, and she was attracted to a guide dog both as a safety tool, like her cane, but also as a source of reassurance and comfort—a service animal and an emotional support animal, all in one.

Kate practiced her cane skills—you have to be an expert with the long white cane before you're allowed to apply for a dog—and after she passed the required test, she was partnered with a golden retriever named Cabot, whom she described as an "incredible friend, companion, and guide." While Kate had grown up with pets, she told me that the bond with a guide dog is entirely different. A family pet's attention is often divided among several people, but a guide dog has just one provider, attention giver, feeder, and petter, and that person and that dog are together 24/7. The connection really seems to be on a different level. Kate's experience with Cabot is far from unique—so many people have had their lives fundamentally changed for the better after developing a relationship with a service animal.

I had the chance to shadow one such pair, Andrew Johnson and his Seeing Eye dog, Gene, on a spring day in 2021. Gene is a chocolate Lab, bred and trained by the Seeing Eye organization, in Morristown, New Jersey. While people often use the terms *Seeing Eye dog* and *guide dog* interchangeably, technically only dogs from the Seeing Eye are official Seeing Eye dogs. I met Andrew and Gene outside their home in Watertown, Massachusetts, and we walked three quarters of a mile down the road to a coffee shop to talk. Even before Gene was in his official Seeing Eye harness, he swiftly led Andrew down the five steps from the front porch. Gene greeted me like any sweet chocolate Lab would—lots of big sniffs and tail wags—but once Andrew slipped the harness over the dog's head, we were off. And we were off *fast*. "With Gene I can finally walk as fast as I've always wanted to," Andrew told me over his right shoulder. Gene hugged his left side, and Andrew asked that I walk behind and to the right so as not to distract Gene while he worked. Andrew was born without sight because of a genetic disorder, and he started using a homemade trapezoid-shaped PVC cane when he was two years old. He'd been interested in the idea of a guide dog, but for close to three decades, Andrew continued to use a cane. He was a professional athlete, a five-time member of the US national rowing team, and a competitor in the 2012 Paralympics in London, so he was traveling a lot. "I was also young and staying out late," Andrew laughed. The circumstances didn't feel right for a dog for a while. But then in fall 2018, as he settled into his late twenties, Andrew decided it was time. He submitted his application to the Seeing Eye, and in May 2019, he headed to Morristown for training and to meet Gene.

Walking with Gene and Andrew down Mount Auburn Street—I had to hurry to keep up—I would have guessed the pair had been together a lot longer than two years. "I've gotten to a place with Gene that I've never gotten to with any dance partner in my entire history," Andrew told me over our fancy coffees. On our walk to and from the coffee shop, Gene would occasionally get distracted—he loves babies in strollers and always wants to pull Andrew into the playground on the corner of Arlington Street—but with gentle steering of the harness or a few stern words, Andrew could always quickly get Gene back on track.

At each intersection, Gene would stop at the curb cut, and Andrew would extend his foot to feel for the edge of the sidewalk. Once we had the walk signal — or when, at an intersection without a light, Andrew didn't hear any cars coming — he would tell Gene to go forward, and the two would confidently forge ahead. A few times, Gene did not move when Andrew commanded him onward, because he saw a car or bicycle or pedestrian that Andrew did not. This is called intelligent disobedience.

"It's really a fifty-fifty partnership," Andrew stressed. "There is a bunch of stuff the dog does really well, but then there is stuff that I need to drive the bus on. You have to have a bit of a conversation through the harness, through your voice, through your posture, all these things. You have a conversation with the dog and work it out." At one point on our walk, the three of us approached a sign that had fallen down near the entrance to a parking lot. At first it seemed as if Gene was going to walk Andrew right into it, and I was about to speak up when Gene stopped. Andrew tugged the harness a bit, to tell Gene he wanted to keep moving, and Gene gently tugged back but toward the left, to steer Andrew around the obstacle. Andrew followed the dog's direction, and in seconds they were around the broken sign and sprinting ahead. "There are people with all the good intentions in the world, who try to jump in and help," Andrew told me. "But it's actually very important for me and Gene to make mistakes and learn from them."

After Andrew gushed about Gene for the better part of two hours, I finally asked him if he'd ever go back to using a cane or if he was a dog person for good. What was he going to do when . . . you know. (Despite the topic of my research, I still hate asking about this directly.) Andrew assured me he's a "guide dog user now." He will definitely get another one, and he also wants to do everything in his power to keep Gene with him after he inevitably has to retire.

In general, guide dogs don't live as long as pet dogs—apparently the stress of decision-making wears on them. But guide dogs keep working until they can't anymore, retiring only once they get too old or if they develop a physical or cognitive issue or are suffering from a lot of pain. Some people choose to keep their retired guide dogs as pets, but that isn't always an option. Landlords have to allow their tenants to have service animals if they need them, but if that guide dog is demoted to pet status? The landlord can evict you. There's also the question of money: if you partner with a new guide dog after your first retires, the financial responsibility of caring for multiple dogs—especially if one is old and sick—can be too much. And psychologically, it can be hard on retired guide dogs when they're unable to work anymore, especially when they're around their person. They don't understand why they're suddenly being left behind. Andrew said his hope is to own his own place by the time Gene has to retire, so the landlord factor won't be an issue, but if it is, Andrew said, he already got his parents to promise to take on Gene as a pet.

Kate, unfortunately, already had to go through all of this with Cabot, who got cancer when he was six and had to retire. Kate adopted Cabot out to a family she knew because she felt it wasn't fair to keep him at home alone all day, especially while she went out with her new guide dog, a black Lab named Hosta. "The dog's whole life has had purpose," Kate said. "The dog puts on a harness and does a job. To be without the harness—it can be devastating for the dog." Cabot died not too long after he retired, and Kate put together a box of his things—collar, leash, and other items that she can touch and be reminded of him.

When I spoke with Kate in April 2019, she told me that she felt her bond with Hosta was so strong that she didn't think she could get another guide dog after her: "I can't bear the idea of replacing her." When Kate and I talked on the phone, she was at work—she's the assistant director of college success at the Perkins School for the Blind—and Hosta was snoozing on her dog bed in Kate's office. ("Counting down the minutes to dinner, I'm sure.") At the time, Hosta was ten, and Kate said she still could have the energy of a puppy, especially in the instant that Kate would put on her harness. But Hosta was starting to slow down. She had been trained as a walking and running guide dog, but now when Kate ran triathlons, she used a (human) running guide. She was also using her cane more and more, to give Hosta a break when she would get tired, and Kate told me she had decided that when Hosta needed to retire, she would live out the rest of her life with Kate as a pet, and Kate would rely on her cane. Kate told me she was willing to sacrifice having a new guide dog until Hosta's death, to allow the dog a happy retirement by her person's side. Unfortunately, Hosta didn't get many retirement years—she died about a year and a half after Kate and I spoke, and the experience was so painful for Kate that it was difficult for her to reply to my messages about Hosta afterward. She did eventually get another guide dog—an "incredibly silly yellow Labrador" named Dodger—which, I like to think, is what Cabot and Hosta would have wanted her to do.

Maybe there is something too special about the bond with a pet, something too essential about the support they give us, to give up on it—to never love again. My first and only (as of this writing) canine student was a goldador (half golden retriever, half Lab) named Orda. During our three-hour creative writing classes, Orda lay silently under the table in his blue vest, reminding the group of his presence only when he shifted his position with the slight clank of his collar. Orda is the service animal of one of my students, Francis—a photographer, writer, and retired US Army veteran who fought in two wars and covered a third as a journalist—and until I spent three hours a week with them for six weeks, I don't think I fully appreciated the bond between a service animal and its human. "We go everywhere together," Francis said, "a married couple in love."

Orda is trained to assist Francis in several ways. When Francis collapsed from low blood pressure, Orda stood strong and still so he could use the dog as a brace to stand up. If Francis finds himself in a crowded space and feels a PTSD episode coming on, Orda can sweep the area in front of him, clearing away other people, giving Francis a protective bubble of space. When I visited Francis and Orda at their apartment in North Quincy ("Pardon the mess," Francis said; "two guys live here") a year after our class, Francis released Orda from his service to bound down the hallway of the building to greet me like any other good boy. But as Francis, Orda, and I sat together talking and catching up, I noticed that the dog's attention was always trained on Francis, even when I was scratching his face and chin. If Francis got up to use the bathroom or to make coffee in the kitchen, Orda kept his eyes on the doorway. And whenever Francis returned, I could feel the warmth between these two guys. Because that's really how they seemed: just two guys helping each other out, making sure they both made it through the day.

A few days after my visit with Francis and Orda, I got a text from Francis saying that the two of them had completed 2.5 miles of walking every day for thirty days in a row, just in time for their fourth anniversary together, October 17, 2020. He told me that nothing could stop them — not bad weather, not health issues, not a global pandemic — and that they kept it up thanks to determination and partnership. Making every moment count, just like Andrew and Gene or Kate and Hosta. "What a gift he is to life," Francis added.

Life is full of shit. Francis knows this. He's lived through some extraordinarily hard things. When Orda dies, it will be another experience of great pain for him, I know. But as my friend Dr. Alli Coates, a veterinarian in western Massachusetts, has said, having a pet is "a microcosm of all life experience. It has an exciting beginning and a sad end. Whether it's college or camp or a romantic partnership or a pet." Or, to quote a classic from Alfred, Lord Tennyson: "'Tis better to have loved and lost than never to have loved at all."

Rodents & Responsibility

*I*N THE FALL OF 1997, I left the iguanas at Montessori and started fourth grade at a new school. Making human friends when you're nine years old and feel more comfortable around animals is hard. I was shy. During recess I hung back from the four-square courts, the center of all the school drama. I got a stomachache before sleepovers and usually bailed last minute. But then one day, during homeroom, our fourth-grade teacher suggested we go around and name our dream pet, if we could have any animal in the world. My head spun as my classmates named off breeds of dogs, exotic cats, fancy horses — I'd fantasized about having just about every kind of pet at one point or another.

"E.B.?" my teacher asked.

"Oh, um . . ." My brain suddenly recalled photos I'd seen recently on an AOL animal message board of a pair of ferrets lounging in a hammock. I'd been reading about them ever since.

"A ferret!" I replied. I waited for the *aww*s that had greeted everyone else's responses, but instead: crickets.

"My sister has ferrets," someone offered. "They smell really bad."

"You know," a sweet, freckly girl named Meri said. "I've always wanted a ferret, too." My focus lasered in on her, and she smiled at me. I felt my panic dissipate. It was the same feeling I got when I came home from school and greeted my pets—completely at ease, relaxed, calm. Maybe this girl . . . could be my friend?

I found Meri later at recess and we started exchanging ferret facts, and then other animal knowledge in general, and then suddenly Meri was inviting me to play four square with her and her friends and I was going to sleepovers at her house and I didn't really get a stomachache anymore. Finding a human friend I could talk to *about* my animal friends felt right. By the end of fourth grade, Meri and I were tight. And while neither of us had gotten a ferret by then, Meri had adopted an orange-and-white hamster named Chuckie.

Chuckie was already a couple of years old, well past hamster middle age, plus he'd had a hard life before he arrived at Meri's, living with a boy who liked to jump over the squirmy, scrawny fistful of fur with his skateboard. Perhaps foreshadowing her future career as a nurse-midwife,

Meri took Chuckie in and showered him with love and care, a hamster death doula easing him through old age. In no time at all, he'd fattened up and calmed down; his favorite activity was rolling around on the floor inside a transparent blue ball. Everything was perfect until spring break the following year, when we were in fifth grade and Meri and her parents went on vacation to Orlando and left Chuckie with me for safekeeping.

For three days it was a montage of fun and frolicking with good old Chuckie. Mom was so impressed with the care I bestowed on the rodent that she even said I might be able to get my own hamster. But then, on the morning of the fourth day, when I went to pick Chuckie up out of his terrarium, he didn't move. And he was cold.

I ripped my hand out of the tank and screamed for my parents.

"Well," said my mother once she'd assessed the situation, "I know what we're not going to do. We're not going to tell Meri about this until she gets back. Her parents paid a lot of money to take her to Disney World, and we're not going to ruin their vacation. Got it?"

My father shrugged. I nodded glumly.

"Now, Elizabeth, help me clean out this tank. Rich, put the hamster on ice."

My stomach churned as my dad gently scooped up Chuckie and packed him away in a plastic bag in a cooler in the garage. I helped my mom scrape out the wood chips and wash out the tank. Losing any pet was sad, but there was something more pressing on my mind: Chuckie wasn't just any pet; he was my friend's pet. What was I going to tell Meri? And was this my fault? That same old sleepover stomachache feeling was back.

Every time the phone rang the rest of that week, I jumped. Twice a day for three days we managed to avoid Meri's calls. (Thank God for those early days of caller ID.)

But eventually I had to own up to the truth. Meri called as soon as she and her parents landed at Logan.

"E.B.! Hi! We're back! When can we come by to pick up Chuckie?"

I gripped the thick black plastic phone in my right hand, the coiled line wrapped around and around my left, squeezing it so tight the cord made an impression on my palm.

"E.B.? You still there?"

"Yes, Meri. I'm sorry." My eyes started to well. I was certain this would be the last time Meri would ever speak to me.

"Sorry?"

"Well, see, while you were away, I mean, I followed all of your instructions so carefully, I really did, and I think it was just because he was old and . . ."

"What happened?"

I inhaled. Dad gave a supportive nod. Mom grimaced.

"Chuckie died."

"What?" Meri shrieked and dropped the phone. I heard a muffled exchange, sobs, and then Meri's mom, Dori, came on the line.

"E.B., can you give the phone to your mom?" she said.

I thrust the phone at Mom, ran into the family room, and threw myself onto the sofa, burrowing into the cushions and fleece blankets. This was the end. I knew it. Meri would never speak to me again. I was the worst friend a girl could have.

But she did speak to me. Not even forty-eight hours later, on the first day back at school, there was Meri, asking if I wanted to play four square, telling me about her plans for her upcoming birthday party, eventually even joking about how Chuckie was still in the freezer by the Brigham's ice cream because the spring soil was too hard to bury him. I was shocked. I had handed the girl's pet back to her in a plastic bag full of ice, and somehow Meri was never anything but kind, understanding, and graceful. "I mean," she would say years later, "that hamster was at his life expectancy when we left." And indeed, decades later, we are still friends. The dead hamster only brought us closer.* Meri

---

* Also, it should be noted that in the wake of Chuckie's death, Meri's parents got her a West Highland white terrier named Jasper, so, in a way, Meri really owes me one.

understood something that I hadn't understood myself, or hadn't let myself understand because I was too busy beating myself up, thinking of all the ways I must have messed up. No, Meri got it: I had done the best I could.

When you think about what it really means to have a pet, there's something kind of ridiculous about it. *Here, let me take this being, from an entirely separate species, that does not speak my language, that has completely distinct needs and wants, a totally different understanding of the world than I do, and let me care for it for the entirety of its life.* It's a lot of pressure. Dave Madden puts it well in *The Authentic Animal:* "As any pet person knows what creates the love between the human and the pet is the notion of custody. *This animal's life is my responsibility.* Every loss of every pet is met with some anxious mix of deprivation and personal shame." The responsibilities of having a pet are similar to the responsibilities of caring for a child: providing nourishment, taking them to the doctor when necessary, giving entertainment, showering with affection. But pets never move out of the house. They don't go off to college and start taking care of themselves. They're dependent on you for as long as they live. As my friend Matt pointed out, for him, his cat Minnie will be only one part of his life, but for Minnie, Matt is her entire life. It's a lot of responsibility, and inevitably you'll mess some of it up. And with creatures so very dependent on you, it's hard not to feel shame and guilt when they die, even if you had no hand in their death at all.

Some people do inadvertently cause a pet's death — I must admit, until I started writing this book, I had no idea just how many people have a story about a violent and traumatic pet death that was directly caused by them or a family member: a childhood gerbil getting sucked up by a vacuum or a new kitten run over by a distracted parent in a car. I also hadn't realized how many of my fellow pet caretakers obsess over the potential death of a pet, picturing their dog running into the street after the mail truck, or a slow, inevitable decline from feline leukemia. Anything can happen, and you won't know what until it does.

Because even with the best care, the best of intentions, accidents happen. Sy Montgomery writes in *The Soul of an Octopus* about Bill Murphy, senior aquarist at the New England Aquarium, in Boston, who has spent his whole career making sure the octopuses at the aquarium have the best possible lives. When the aquarium's baby octopus, Kali, grew too big for her enclosure, Murphy transferred her to another tank with more space. But she was able to escape and died, drying out on the floor in front of her tank. "That such a meticulous, caring man has lost the most intelligent, outgoing, and beloved of them all — and worst, lost her, he believes, because of his mistake — seems brutally, cosmically wrong," writes Montgomery. "Bill's sorrow sweeps over my own like a sob." The ironic part about Kali's death is that she may have died from coming into contact with the mat on the floor, treated with the solution Virkon, which kills viruses, bacteria, and fungi. "The irony is almost too painful to bear," writes Montgomery. "Kali escaped because those who loved her most were trying to give her the best life possible, and may have died because of their efforts to protect their animals from danger and disease." We try so hard, but the truth is that we're clumsy animals ourselves. Humans can't predict or prepare for everything—or anything, really—but there's something about our role as protectors and caretakers that makes us feel a particularly deep guilt in our failures.

And there are so many differently heartbreaking ways to feel like you've failed. My friend told me about her aunt who was devastated when she had to euthanize her dog because she couldn't afford the surgery that could have saved his life. Another friend of a friend was carrying a basket of laundry and accidentally knocked a chair over that severely injured her Senegal parrot, Darzee, which ultimately led to his death. Some people deny or ignore symptoms of a pet's illness until it's too late.

And sometimes you actively give up on your pet.

Back in fifth grade, Mom felt bad enough about the Chuckie Incident that for approximately ten days, in the spring of 1999, I ended up with a guinea pig named Felix.

I think Mom knew that I felt responsible for Chuckie's demise, and she thought that the best way to heal the wound of one pet dying was by welcoming home a new one. (A vicious cycle.) But more importantly, I also think that the guinea pig was supposed to feel like a fresh start. A chance for me to prove to myself that I could actually take care of a little rodent friend — that Chuckie really had died of old age, that his death was inevitable and it just happened to come when he was under my care. But it didn't quite work out like that.

Felix the guinea pig is one of my shameful secrets. Most of my friends don't know I ever had him. Until now, I've avoided talking about him at all costs.

Here's what happened. I went with my mom to Petco in Burlington and picked out a dark brown guinea pig with an orange stripe around his middle, like a Halloween-edition Oreo. I named him Felix. I brought him home. And he proceeded to bite the shit out of me. I was shocked — it was the first time in my life that I'd had trouble handling an animal. Every time I tried to lift him out of the tank to play, he would lunge at my thumb. It was impossible to clean his tank. I tried petting him. I tried speaking to him. I tried hanging out near his enclosure so he could get used to me. Nothing worked. And so I gave up. With every other pet I'd had, it was till-death-do-us-part. But with Felix, I failed at my responsibilities as a pet caretaker.

I became afraid of him and then neglected him. I stopped cleaning his cage because he would attack me so viciously. I would throw his food into his enclosure without even stopping to look at him. I started trying to avoid the part of the house where his tank was, which was hard, considering it was in the hallway to the back door. When I did have to walk by Felix, I kept my eyes down — the shame and guilt were too much to bear. I had genuinely been trying my best with Chuckie, but with Felix I wasn't trying at all anymore. When Mom finally took matters into her own hands and returned the guinea pig to Petco, I don't think we even fought about it. I was resigned.

When Mom came back from Petco — I didn't even go with her, I was so ashamed — she told me that it had been no problem. She was able to give the guinea pig back to the store and there was actually a woman there looking for a guinea pig who took Felix home. This woman was experienced with guinea pigs, my mom assured me; she would be able to train him and take care of him. I wasn't completely sure I believed her story. I wanted to, but part of me wondered if the Petco employees hadn't just taken Felix to the back and euthanized him. Deep down, I knew this was the more likely story, and I feel bad about it to this day.

Some people have difficult and tragic reasons for needing to surrender a pet — a dog that turns aggressive toward a new baby, an international move, dire financial circumstances, entering assisted living, a prolonged illness — and others give up, like I did with Felix, because it's just too hard. All kinds of people love animals, but not everyone understands the amount of effort and work that goes into caring for them. How many little kids beg for a kitten or a puppy, only to have the adults in the house end up taking care of the pet? I'm also remembering how in the early 2000s tons of people adopted Chihuahuas like Paris Hilton's, only to surrender them to shelters after getting sick of having a small dog around. And how every year, about a month after Easter, animal shelters see an influx of rabbits that were given as cute Easter Bunny gifts, only to have kids become bored with them after a couple weeks.

In the spring of 2020, at the start of the COVID-19 pandemic, animal shelters all across the United States saw the opposite issue: they were depleted of pets. It seems everyone adopted a coronavirus puppy or kitten in March or April 2020. Shelters that usually had pages and pages and pages of animals available for adoption were down to one or two listings, and even those were usually already on hold for someone else by the time you called the shelter to inquire. If you were trying to adopt an animal during COVID, you pretty much had to be comfortable with taking in whatever you could get. Pet stores couldn't stock product fast enough. Dog training classes were selling out. Parks exploded with puppies.

That's the good news. But a lot of veterinarians I interviewed for this book expressed concern that after the pandemic, when people return to being out of the house for eight to ten hours a day, they aren't going to want to deal with the responsibility of finding a dog walker or signing a pup up for daycare, and the shelters will fill back up.

But often with pets even doing your best still isn't good enough, or at least it doesn't feel like it. Decisions about their welfare and happiness are never clean or easy. How can a human ever really understand what's going on in a guinea pig's head? You can't. And here's the great pet paradox — even if you don't neglect your pet, like I did during my brief guinea pig experience, even if you do everything in your power to let your pet have the best possible life, like Meri did with Chuckie — no matter how well you care for them, at the end of the day, most of us still end up being directly responsible for our pets' deaths through euthanasia. Sure, these days most pet people aren't the ones pulling the trigger, à la *Old Yeller,* but more often than not, we make the call.

It's tricky to locate statistics on this. The Humane Society of the United States estimates that of the six to eight million cats and dogs that end up in shelters every year, three to four million are euthanized, but statistics on how many pets are euthanized at veterinary clinics or at home are harder to find. "All we know for sure," writes Jessica

Pierce in her book *The Last Walk,* "is that far more die by the needle than by natural causes." Very few pets, it seems, die on their own these days. In a study of 305 pet people, nearly 70 percent chose to euthanize their pet at the end.

But how exactly do you decide it's time? Animals can't tell you. They can show you — by not drinking water, by not eating, by losing interest in their favorite activities — but you can never know for sure. So many pet people desperately wish for someone or something else to tell them when to make the decision. Dr. Alli Coates told me that when she was in veterinary school at Tufts, she was taught to tell her clients to "think of three things your pet loves to do, and if they can't do those things anymore — go for walks, swim in a lake, chase a ball — it's probably time to euthanize." Another veterinarian I spoke with, Dr. Bennett King, who was still a veterinary student at the time of our conversation, told me that one of her classes at the University of Pennsylvania was taught by a grief counselor who coached them on helping people navigate the deaths of their animals and how to talk to children about it. So much of vet school, King said, was talking about how to know if it's the right time to put down an animal.

But, as Dr. Suzy Fincham-Gray writes in her book *My Patients and Other Animals,* "The expertise needed to counsel a grieving client, find the right words to explain a complicated disease to a layperson, or understand that a person's anger was often a manifestation of fear, were not requirements for graduation." Even practicing with actors, as many vet schools now require, can't quite prepare you for the real thing.

Every situation and every pet is different, and no one knows your animal like you do. The timing is something you have to figure out for yourself, and that doesn't make it any easier. "It's always too late or too soon," said Unitarian Universalist minister Eliza Blanchard, who runs a pet-loss healing circle at a Boston-area parish. Many people put off even considering euthanasia for as long as they can — perhaps as a coping mechanism, a way to deny the animal's coming death. Euthanasia is often seen as the absolute last resort. People want to make sure they've exhausted every other possibility before even thinking about the needle.

Part of me wonders if this is because people care what other people think — they don't want to be seen as someone who "gave up" too quickly on their pet, jumping to euthanasia to avoid a hard, sad, and expensive decline. But so many pet caretakers I've spoken with have told me that only long after their pet had died did they realize how much they'd dragged out their animal's suffering and pain, simply because they didn't want to let go. Even with Coates's "three things," there are good days and bad days. It's easy to focus on the good days, to use them to convince yourself that it isn't time yet. And of course, animals have evolved to hide signs of illness or pain. Showing weakness turns an animal into prey in the wild. Most pets actively try not to show us if they are hurt or ill—which is why often, by the time humans notice any symptoms, the animal is critically and fatally sick.

Euthanasia wasn't always seen as a last resort—the thinking around it has changed with time. People used to make the choice to euthanize a lot sooner than most do now. I spoke with an equine vet, Dr. Stephen Carr, at the Saratoga Race Course in summer 2017. Carr has been a vet for forty years. "Initially animals were not viewed so much as pets but as helpers," he told me. In the 1940s, he explained, no one would hesitate to euthanize an injured horse, because repairing its injury would be too expensive or too painful for the animal. And, more important, even if the horse could recover from an injury, if she wouldn't be able to race anymore, most trainers wouldn't see any point in keeping her alive. "But now a lot more people question euthanizing an animal," Carr said. All the advances in medicine have allowed veterinarians to cure conditions that would have been hopeless in the past and keep more horses alive than they used to. With that opportunity comes obligation. And our sense of animals as purely utilitarian is less and less widespread.

To state the obvious: veterinarians don't enjoy euthanizing animals. We were sitting in Carr's truck as we had this conversation, and one of Saratoga's horse ambulances drove by, coming back from the racecourse. Carr peered into the ambulance as it passed. "Oh, good," he said. "You always want to see it empty." While euthanasia is part of the veterinary profession, the hope is always to heal — most vets become vets because they want to help pets, not end their lives.

But a lot of the work that comes with being a vet might not be what one expects. I spoke with Dr. Indu Mani, a vet at an animal hospital in Brookline, Massachusetts, who observed that many people go into veterinary practice because they love animals and want to work with them, not quite realizing that taking care of animals requires taking care of those animals' people, too. It reminded me of when I first started teaching middle school: the summer before school started, I was so worried about doing right by my students as I prepared for their classes, but come September, I was completely blindsided by how many hours I had to spend consoling and counseling their parents, too. No one warned me about that part of the job. And many vets seem to feel more comfortable with animals than with humans, and yet every day they have to have really difficult conversations with . . . humans.

Mani pointed out that no human doctors care for their patients all the way from birth through old age, but veterinarians often do. "Being a pediatrician and gerontologist all in one is a tough place to dwell," she said. I've always been impressed by the number of different species and breeds whose anatomy and health risks veterinarians have to know—human doctors have it easy by comparison, just dealing with *Homo sapiens*. But I hadn't really thought about how human medicine is also divided up into such individualized specialties that many human doctors need to be experts only in the part of the species they work on. Specialists, likewise, are becoming more prevalent in veterinary medicine—in veterinary school, students often choose to focus on studying small animals (dogs and cats), large animals (horses and livestock), or exotics (reptiles, birds, your goth friend's tarantula), and now there are also behaviorists, oncologists, cardiologists, dermatologists, orthopedists, dentists, ophthalmologists—you name it—for pets.

But regardless of specialty, regardless of species, if a veterinarian has to talk to a person about their pet, hard conversations are going to happen. Is it worth it to spend $10,000 on a surgery that might extend your dog's life by only a couple of months? Can you even afford it? Some people argue that it's heartless not to try to do everything to save your pet, regardless of money—you'd spend $10,000 to extend your grandmother's life, so why not your dog's? Others argue it's ludicrous to spend so much money on an animal—it's your dog, not your grandmother. Some people would love to spend whatever it takes to help their pet but simply can't afford to do so. Others feel you shouldn't have a pet in the first place if you can't afford those kinds of payments. There are people who think it's cruel to subject a pet to a painful surgery or treatment like chemo if it's not going to completely cure them or extend their life by much, especially since you can't explain to a pet patient what's going on the way you can with a human patient. And yet others see euthanasia as the (relatively) cheap and easy way out. There are so many highly contradictory perspectives, and veterinarians are the ones who have to guide people through them. Another vet I spoke with, Dr. Katie Moynihan, said that she receives a lot of "redirected aggression" from upset or distressed clients. "That's a term we use for cats with behavioral issues, but it also applies to humans," she explained. "The vet is just delivering the bad news. There's a lot of shooting the messenger."

Susan P. Cohen noticed this type of tension and nervousness between clients and vets when she was at an animal hospital—as a client. Cohen has a doctorate in social welfare, and once, when she was bringing her cat to the vet and realizing just how nervous she felt being there, worrying about her pet, it occurred to her that animal hospitals should have someone like a social worker present— someone to help translate medical phrases into common language, to help talk through difficult decisions, to assist in weighing the pros and cons. Human hospitals are full of resources for emotional support; why shouldn't animal hospitals have the same? And, Cohen thought, in an animal hospital you might need even more—someone specifically trained in human mental health and well-being, not just pet health and well-being. Cohen approached the Animal Medical Center, in New York City, about the possibility—a "Mayo Clinic for pets"—and they were willing to try it out. She wrote the job description herself, and figured out how to tweak and adjust things over the course of the twenty-eight years she spent in the role. Ultimately, she found that she was providing support not just for her clients but also to the vets—helping them see the people, not just the pets. "Vets are often looking at the pet and not at the person at all, and they get annoyed that the pet owner is chatting their ear off," explained Cohen. "The owner isn't chatting because they're lonely, but because it's helping them make a decision." Cohen became the person to help clients make those decisions, to talk through their thoughts, and also to support vets by helping them explain difficult things. She also promoted transparency between vets and clients. "For a long time, vets told clients that they couldn't be present for their pet's euthanasia. The theory was that the clients would be so shocked by what happened that they'd faint and hit their heads and sue," Cohen sighed, exasperated. "So I said, 'Okay, well, then let's get them a chair and some Kleenex and tell them what's going to happen first.'" I laughed, but it made sense—vets are also people, afraid of making mistakes, not wanting to hurt other people. And if many vets are "proud introverts" (as Cohen put it), leaving the people on the other side of the door is probably their most comfortable instinct in a challenging situation.

The toll of being a vet can be heavy. Mani said that one of the most frustrating and upsetting things she has to deal with as a vet is when she knows there's a treatment option for an animal, but the animal's caretaker can't afford it. Several vets I spoke with expressed this sentiment, wishing they could provide lifesaving services at no cost. "But we can't do care for free," Mani said with a heavy sigh. "If we don't charge for our services, we can't do our services."

Money is something that weighs heavily on veterinarians in a way that it doesn't always on human doctors. So many more humans have medical insurance than pets, and even humans without medical insurance can sometimes receive treatment at hospitals that have policies not to refuse care. Physicians are not trained to think or talk through the cost of treatments with patients in the same way vets are; instead, human doctors are taught to try every possible treatment, because in their field euthanasia is not an option. Money is not supposed to be a factor when thinking about treating people. Insanely pricey surgery?

Expensive weekly chemo? Casts, braces, physical therapy, medicine? Physicians are ethically obligated to try it all, and they can send the bill to the insurance company (or burden a patient with enormous medical debt). But sometimes, as Coates pointed out, this makes human doctors almost a little too ready to treat, no matter the circumstances. I think of cancer patients I knew who were still getting radiation right up to the week of their death, their doctors "fighting" the disease so hard that they were denying to themselves and to the patient and to the patient's family that death was coming, no matter how many procedures they tried. Because pet insurance has become more common only recently — and because pet insurance covers even less than human insurance generally does — vets have to have the hard talks with pet caretakers about cost and benefits. Is it worth $10,000 to extend your dog's life by a week? A month? A year?

It's no wonder so many vets suffer from compassion fatigue — the emotional or physical exhaustion that comes from having to constantly practice empathy. Nonstop professional empathy can actually lead to indifference or a diminished ability to feel compassion. That's why there is so much burnout in the field of veterinary medicine — a lot of vets do it for a decade or so and then need to pivot into research or teaching. Working day-to-day in a practice is just so hard.

Veterinarians can graduate with anywhere from $100,000 to $500,000 in debt, but veterinarian salaries remain low enough that paying it off can be difficult, even impossible. (In Ontario, Donna Ross and her husband, Peter Szmidt, chose to honor their deceased dog, Dalwood, by starting a scholarship for vet students at the University of Guelph, to help alleviate this enormous debt: the Dalwood Memorial Scholarship.) Mix that financial stress with compassion fatigue, working long hours, the isolation of small practices, and frequently getting harassed and bullied by upset clients—it's a daunting combination. And death is ever present in the work of a veterinarian; more than any other healthcare professional, vets are present at the deaths of their patients—about five times more often. They're also often forced to act as undertaker.

In January 2019, the Centers for Disease Control and Prevention released the results of the first study to examine veterinarian mortality rates in the United States, and the results were alarming: between 1979 and 2015, male veterinarians committed suicide twice as often as the national average, and female vets 3.5 times as often. A 2015 CDC study found that one in six veterinarians have considered suicide. Nearly every single veterinarian I spoke with for this book referenced the high rate of suicide among their colleagues.

Dr. Suzanne Tomasi, the lead author of the 2019 CDC

study, points out that veterinarians are more likely to be successful in their suicide attempts, because they have access to lethal drugs and they know how to properly administer them. Most human doctors are not trained to kill. Dr. Philip Bergman, a veterinary oncologist, has known three fellow oncologists who have taken their own lives, plus a classmate in vet school. "Veterinary medicine tends to attract incredibly intelligent people with a high IQ but often with a low EQ," Bergman explained. EQ, or emotional quotient, measures a person's ability to identify and manage their own emotions and also the emotions of others. It seems that a lot of vets are not ready for the great burden and responsibility of the emotional toll of the profession. King shared that over and over in vet school, her professors stressed to her and her classmates, "You can't take on other people's grief."

Easier said than done, of course. "I still cry at euthanasias," said Mani, who has been a vet for twenty-five years. Bergman teared up over Zoom when he told me about one canine patient who had passed whose owner chose to scatter some of the dog's ashes on the grounds of the animal hospital. "Part of him needs to stay here," the owner explained, grateful for all the treatments and support Bergman had given her dog. It was the first time one of his clients had done that. Another equine vet I spoke with, Dr. Sandi Farris, who lives and practices on Whidbey Island,

Washington, explained just how physically difficult and graphic performing euthanasia can be, especially on a large animal. When it comes to horse and farm animal euthanasia, there's no room with soft lighting — nothing about it is "quiet or dainty," as Farris put it. Sometimes she can manipulate a horse to sit down before she euthanizes so they have a shorter distance to fall, or she can get them to lie down using chemicals. "Twelve hundred pounds hitting the ground makes a big, ugly noise," Farris said. In particular, she tries to make sure the horse's head doesn't hit the ground when the owner is present. When she said this, my stomach rolled as I pictured a horse skull smashing into the ground from six feet up. But then I thought about what a kindness it was for Farris to try to protect her clients from seeing that, what a kind act she's performing in general.

Because that's really what euthanasia is: an act of kindness. "I see euthanasia as a blessing," Bergman said. "It allows us to prevent suffering." Farris referred to it as "a gift we can give our animals." And Moynihan said that most vets she knows think of euthanasia as a positive thing they can do for animals. "If we find out an animal has passed on their own, we almost feel like we failed," she said. She explained that she feels like she could have eased the animal's final minutes but was not able to do so. Clients usually feel relieved about a natural death — it eliminates the painful decision-making — but Moynihan said this makes vets feel guilty. Mani said the same thing: "I feel responsible to give the animal the best death they can, just like I feel responsible to give the animal the best life they can."

The word *euthanasia* comes from the Greek *euthanatos,* meaning "good death." In *The Unbearable Lightness of Being,* Kundera writes, "Dogs do not have many advantages over people, but one of them is extremely important: euthanasia is not forbidden by law in their case; animals have the right to a merciful death." Sometimes I wonder why we can give this opportunity to our nonhuman family members but not our human ones, especially since those humans have the language to communicate with us what they want. Farris said one of her clients brought her sick animal to be euthanized and said, "I don't want him to suffer like my mom did." She sighed after telling me this, saying, "It's crazy what we don't provide for our own species." Bergman said that when his grandfather was dying from metastatic prostate cancer and in horrific pain, he said to him, "I don't understand why you can euthanize dogs but you can't do that with me."

Of course, vets are human, and euthanasia isn't perfect. Animals can gasp, vocalize, or twitch during or just after death, which can be traumatic for the people in the room. The veins on an old animal are often hard to locate, which can draw out the whole process, and sometimes the animal requires more euthanasia solution than was calculated based on the usual metrics. In fact, King was partly inspired to attend vet school after watching a difficult euthanasia. She grew up with a Bernese mountain dog named Gabby, and when Gabby eventually became old and sick, her family decided to euthanize. But Gabby was so old that her veins were weak; it took the vet a while to find a good one. Then, after that, the sedative and euthanasia solution took an extra-long time to kick in — King realizes now that it might have been because the solution was injected outside of the dog's veins, making it harder for her body to absorb. "It was one of the worst euthanasias I've ever seen," she said. We were sitting together at a Thai restaurant as she told me this story, her fork resting next to her plate, her food untouched.

But a seamless euthanasia can create a strong veterinarian-client bond. "Most of the cards you get as a vet are because a client is thanking you for performing a euthanasia," Moynihan said. "People don't send cards because you figured out why their dog has diarrhea." She described one at-home euthanasia she did for longtime clients who had stayed with her when she moved from one animal hospital to another, a few towns west. When she arrived with her veterinarian bag, one of the clients opened the door and said, "We're making pizza, I hope you can stay!" Moynihan euthanized the dog, surrounded by the family, and then she stayed for two hours, eating pizza, drinking wine, and sharing stories about the dog.

The fact that you can plan when a euthanasia will happen, too, means that you can take the time to celebrate your animal with others. If you know the end of your pet's life is coming, you can have a memorial service for him while he's still alive. You can do all sorts of things to make sure your pet feels loved, secure, and happy in his final moments. A friend of a friend grew up with a dog named Seaweed, and when it came time for Seaweed to go, the friend's dad took him to the McDonald's drive-through on the way to the vet. He got the dog three hamburgers and said, "Go to town, Seaweed."

My friends Tuck and Liz's friends had a big party for their dog the night before his death, inviting everyone who had also known and loved their pet; they even dressed the dog up in a tuxedo and top hat for the occasion.

When it became clear that the end was near for her dog Harvey, the writer Annie Hartnett invited friends over for an open house to say goodbye to the border collie. Of course, all of Hartnett's pet-loving friends showed up, but she said it meant the most to her when even a friend who pointedly does not like dogs arrived with cookies and flowers.

My college roommate Lee's family made their thirteen-

and-a-half-year-old German shepherd, Bella, a steak dinner and took her for a drive along the California coast before she was euthanized.

Dr. Dani McVety has built her whole practice around the idea of making the last day a good day. When she was in veterinary school, she discovered that she was particularly skilled at dealing with the end-of-life stuff—she was direct and honest, she didn't sugarcoat, and she found that people responded well to that. She also realized that she was resilient when it came to compassion fatigue.

When I spoke with her on the phone, McVety told me, "I have never felt compassion fatigue doing what I do now—never. I can euthanize nine patients in a day, and each one feels like the first one that I've done." Which is good, because euthanizing nine patients in a day is a regular day for McVety, who runs her own practice now called Lap of Love Veterinary Hospice, in Tampa, Florida. Lap of Love offers hospice care for elderly and sick animals, medical house calls for pets, at-home euthanasia, and even pet aftercare services. "What I do now is help people say goodbye in the most compassionate way," McVety told me. "In human medicine we are taught to *fight, fight, fight,* and one day I thought, *What am I fighting against?*" It's not that she doesn't try to make sick animals well, but because she concentrates on an elderly and dying population, McVety is able to focus on making her patients as comfortable and happy as possible in their final years, months, weeks, days, hours. "I get to treat my patient instead of treating a disease," she explained. Death is part of the life cycle, and McVety tries to help her clients understand that. "Sickness or death doesn't happen because medicine fails you," she said. "It's just a natural progression of biology. Nature does that. We can't prevent sickness and death; we are just here to make the quality of life good. And I am here to make the quality of death very good."

McVety is not the only one drawn to this type of work. Former mortician Ace Tilton Ratcliff and veterinarian Dr. Derek Calhoon started an at-home euthanasia service in Boynton Beach, Florida, called Harper's Promise, named for their now deceased dog Harper. Both Ratcliff and Calhoon believe euthanasia is a gift we can give to our animal friends; as they have written on the Harper's Promise website, "As impossible as it may feel, euthanasia can be the last in a long line of kind and loving decisions you've already made for your pet."

When I spoke on the phone with Ratcliff and Calhoon, one of the first things they emphasized was the importance of their work as a team. Calhoon, as the veterinarian, is the one who has the medical expertise, the one who administers the euthanasia drugs, and the one who wields the final needle. Ratcliff's role is that of a "deathcare adviser." Ratcliff explained, "I'm a layperson, but I have the experience of being chronically ill with a degenerative disease. Because my disease is rare, I've had to do my own medical research and be able to work as a translator." They are able to turn Calhoon's veterinary jargon into simple language that clients can understand; Ratcliff is the one who asks questions, clarifies, and explains as Calhoon does the medical procedures. Ratcliff's work reminded me of Cohen's position at the Animal Medical Center, providing support to both vets and clients at once, and I thought about how much easier, calmer, and better it would have been if I'd had someone like that by my side during the Chuckie Incident. In addition to his at-home euthanasia work through Harper's Promise, Calhoon is a veterinarian at an animal hospital, where he must perform euthanasias on his own, and he said that he misses having someone in Ratcliff's role when dealing in the "traditional, clinical side of euthanasia." The aspect of support and communication is missing in a lot of animal hospitals, with many clinics full of vets who are overworked and lacking resources. But with an at-home euthanasia practice, both vets and clients have all the time and space they need. No colleague is rushing a vet out to use the exam room next, no family with a new puppy is looking at a crying client with a horrified glance, no receptionist is waiting for a credit card as a devastated person sobs. Calhoon and Ratcliff can set the scene and manage the situation and make it as comfortable and private and safe for both the person and the dying animal as possible. When you can plan, your pet can die at home, where they feel the most comfortable and safe—as Ratcliff put it in an essay for *Narratively*, it's "the best way for the worst thing ever to happen."

"The most important thing you can do is set reasonable expectations," explained Calhoon. "The gap between what happened and what was expected needs to be as small as possible. It still sucks, but then at least you're not also dealing with surprise and shock, too." He said that it wasn't until he and Ratcliff had to euthanize Harper that he realized how much of his profession was about helping clients up until the moment of death. For many vets, once the client leaves the room and the patient's body gets sent to the crematorium, that's the end of the support. But the moment of death is when Ratcliff's real work begins. While Calhoon wraps up the physical elements of dying, Ratcliff works on the emotional—encouraging clients to take time with the body, take pictures if they want, to sit and cry and reflect, not to rush. "I think most people misunderstand what 'gaining closure' about a situation means," Calhoon said, explaining that most people assume closure is the end of the feelings, the end of the emotional experience. "But closure is the beginning of the process. Closure is a completeness of perspective, a certainty about the reality about the situation. It closes the event, not the *experience* of the event."

People need different things in order to access closure, and something that Ratcliff and Calhoon often run up against is members of a family wanting or needing different things for the end—for example, a wife who wants to sit with a dog through the euthanasia and long after the dog is gone but whose husband can't bear to be in the room. "I had to tell her it was okay for him to leave," Ratcliff explained. "That he didn't need to grieve in the same way that she did." As soon as the couple heard that, Calhoon said, it was a clear "relief for both of them" and suddenly their focus went from each other to their dying dog. But even professionals have a hard time when it comes to their own animals. Ratcliff and Calhoon showed me photos of a shelf that serves as a shrine to all of their dead pets—collars, paw prints, artwork, photographs, ashes, bones. They both got choked up at different times on our call. Ratcliff told me about the death of their fourteen-year-old dog Roland, who had been with Ratcliff since they were nineteen. Roland had been struggling with a number of health problems for a while, and when it was finally his time to go, Calhoon gave him the smallest possible dosage of euthanasia fluid and it sent him on his way. It was a long weekend and the crematorium was closed. "Roland was the type of dog who was with me wherever I was," Ratcliff explained. So Roland lay in state at home, in a beautiful casket that Calhoon had made, but he didn't lie in one place; Ratcliff moved his body around the house wherever they went for three days. At one point Ratcliff needed to go to the art store to get materials to make a cast of Roland's paw and nose, and Calhoon asked Ratcliff if Roland should come with them. Ratcliff felt overwhelming gratitude for Calhoon in that moment, for understanding that this was part of their grieving process and letting them do what they needed to. "It was a big deal to have your partner be completely okay with driving your dead dog around for three days," Ratcliff said, their words thick with emotion.

Even McVety, who euthanizes animals every day, struggled when her own dog died. She lost the first dog she'd had as an adult when she was three years out of vet school. She'd already started Lap of Love, but still, when it came to the death of her dog, she was hit hard. She felt that she should be handling it better, considering her profession. "I needed me to tell me it was okay," she explained. "I needed to give myself the gift that I give to everyone else."

It's often easier not to do this. It's much easier to blame yourself, be mad at yourself, beat yourself up. I think it's a human thing to focus on the bad, to remember one negative comment in a sea of compliments. It's a place where we should take guidance from our pets. "Dogs are resilient," Mani said, and she's right. Even if a rescue animal has baggage — fears, anxieties, aggression — often they can heal. They can learn to trust and love again.

"We feel so responsible," said Cohen. "We take their death very hard, and we are always full of guilt and regret — *I went to the wrong vet, I had the wrong surgery done, I didn't do enough.*" I nodded as Cohen rattled off so many of the common feelings of pet caretakers in grief. "But I believe in evolution," she went on. "What is the purpose of this terrible grief? Of being haunted by our last view of anyone we care about? It's a protective mechanism, descended from ancestors who paid very close attention to how anyone would become dead or sick, to try to keep it from happening again." It's a natural feeling, and a hard one to shake off. But Cohen encourages grieving pet caretakers to talk to others, perhaps to join a pet-loss support group like the one she runs. "You sit and listen to the guy across from you in the circle tell his story, and he feels terrible guilt, but you think that he did everything he could do, and so you start to think, *Maybe I did everything I could, too. Maybe I don't need to blame myself either,*" Cohen said. "As much as we try, no one has escaped death yet."

There's a saying: "Help me be the person my dog thinks I am." Kind of corny, but I like the sentiment. It's something to aspire to, for sure. But here's the thing: you already are the person your dog (or any other pet) thinks you are.

You give them food and shelter, you throw a tennis ball around, you take them on walks, you scratch their ears, you rub their back, and you love them as much as you can. Those actions may feel simple to you, or you may feel like you're falling short—but those simple things are enough.

I don't think Chuckie is up in hamster heaven, looking down on me, angry that I let him die while Meri was at Disney World. No, I bet that Chuckie was just thrilled that I gave him baby carrots and let him roll around in his blue ball right until the end. Every day, our animals look at us with the love, kindness, and understanding that we need to give to ourselves, especially when it comes to their end-of-life care. So let yourself receive the gift that your pet is giving.

My grandparents' Yorkshire terrier, Samantha, was born in 1971 and lived until she was seventeen years old—we overlapped for seven months during the first half of 1988. When my grandfather, whom I call Puppy, would tell me how Samantha died, all he would say was that she'd had a stroke, was struggling to breathe, and eventually died in his arms. I mean, the dog was seventeen—it made sense. I didn't question it. I pictured my grandfather finding the wheezing Samantha, rushing this tiny dog to the vet, trying to do everything to save her, and finally holding her as she got the euthanasia shot.

"Oh, pal, I didn't take her to the vet," my grandfather

finally told me when I was no longer a child. "Samantha clearly had a stroke, and I picked her up and was holding her in my arms . . ." I pictured my six-foot-something-tall grandfather cradling this four-pound terrier in the crook of his elbow. "Her head was at an angle, and she was gasping and having trouble breathing and . . ." Puppy stopped talking, tears in his eyes. He said he didn't plan it; he said he never would have thought he could do it—he just knew what he needed to do. He gently pet the dog and placed his hand on her neck to see if she would resist. She didn't— and he closed his fingers tighter and tighter. "She knew what was going on," Puppy said, tears streaming. "But she had accepted it. She knew it was the end." Puppy said he cried the whole time. Once Samantha went limp and her bladder released, he knew the little dog was gone. "Be at peace, Sarah Samantha," he said, using her full name. "You were so loved."

More than thirty years later, speaking with me again about Samantha's death, Puppy repeated and repeated, "It was the hardest thing I ever had to do." He never told anyone what he had done. He didn't like to talk about her death at all. He simply said to my grandmother, my mom, and my aunt, and later to me, that Samantha had a stroke and died in his arms. It wasn't not true, but it wasn't the whole truth. "I couldn't tell anyone," Puppy said. "I felt ashamed."

I admit, I was shocked the first time I heard this story —a teenager or perhaps a college student, stunned to learn that my grandfather had killed his own dog. But as I got older, I started to see things differently. My mom pointed out that even though Puppy grew up in the city of Somerville, outside of Boston, he'd had goats and chickens and canaries—a rural kind of lifestyle that perhaps made Puppy more comfortable with hands-on euthanasia. And when you think about it, how is giving your dying Yorkie a final squeeze any different from bringing her to the vet for an injection shot? When I was on the phone with Farris, the equine vet, Samantha came up; I shared how I had struggled to understand how my grandfather had been able to do such a thing.

"Oh," Farris said gently. "That was a kindness." She noted how stressful it would be for a little seventeen-year-old Yorkie to get rushed to an animal hospital—all of those loud noises, the other pets, the chaos. Instead, Samantha died right in my grandfather's arms, the place she loved to be the most. To again paraphrase Milan Kundera, death came for her in the guise of her loved one.

And that is really doing the best we can do.

Turtles & Taxidermy

THE FIRST TIME I saw a dead turtle was in 1999, the summer before I started sixth grade. I was walking along one of the sidewalk-less roads on Fishers Island, the same island where, a few years earlier, I'd thrown Kiki his first birthday party. Fishers has no traffic lights, no hotels, no restaurants, and one bar, and many of the roads are not even paved. It's the sort of place that reminds you how quickly nature can reclaim a space if left to its own devices — sidewalks crack and buckle from tree roots beneath, wisteria and vines quickly cover abandoned structures. And for such a small island, it has a lot of wildlife — bunnies, deer, coyotes, ospreys, feral kittens, one notorious fisher cat, and turtles all the way down.

That fateful day, I was walking on the road next to a shallow body of water nicknamed Scum Pond by my family, for the thick green algae that coats it every summer.

I absentmindedly kicked rocks out of the road and onto the bordering grass. As my foot wound up to kick a particularly flat and odd-shaped rock, I paused for a closer look. Was it a chunk of asphalt? Part of a tire? My breath caught in my throat. It was a baby turtle. A dead baby turtle. It was the size of a Sacagawea dollar, and unnaturally flat—there were tire tracks imprinted on the shell, just like in a cartoon. I went to touch the turtle, to feel the grooves embossed into the carapace, but the body was hot from baking on the July asphalt. I stared in horror: while I had plenty of experience with dead fish, dead birds, and dead hamsters, I'd never seen a dead turtle before. My pet turtles always disappeared on me before they had a chance to die.

Flower Speedy Andersen Bartels was my first. Dad and my brother, Chad, found the eastern painted turtle in the middle of the road on Fishers, the summer I was five years old. Chad, busy with important teenage business, quickly lost interest in the turtle, but I was enamored. Flower spent the summer swimming in a plastic kiddie pool in the driveway, and I gleefully threw her handfuls of raw hamburger meat every morning. It was a glorious time. For me, at least. I'm sure the turtle was miserable.

At the end of the summer, Dad gently tried to explain to me the concept of "temporary pets." He told me that some animals are just visitors, dropping into our lives for a little bit, adding some enjoyment before returning to their real homes in the wild — but I wasn't having it. I convinced my parents to bring Flower back to our house in Lexington and build her a small pond in our yard. But Flower had other ideas. Not even an hour after Dad dug a giant hole in the lawn, submerged a large plastic tub from Home Depot, and surrounded the man-made pond with chicken wire, somehow Flower managed to escape. I was, of course, devastated, just as I'd been about all my other pets. But this time there was no body to bury. Flower wasn't dead; she was just back on her own, somewhere else, without me, which was a confusing kind of grief. While at first this was upsetting, the idea of Flower off having adventures eventually began to bring me some comfort. At least she wasn't dead. At least, if she was dead, I didn't know.

For the turtles that followed Flower — because, of course, there were more turtles — I now got on board with the whole "temporary pets" thing. I had realized that I could outwit the pain and grief of a dead pet by making the choice to let them go. There was the box turtle my grandfather found and named Charlie Brown; a quarter-sized musk turtle my auntie Christine discovered and brought over to our house in a pie dish; another eastern painted turtle from Fishers named Eddie, in honor of the composer Edvard Grieg. There were other turtles, too — some stuck around for just a couple of days, maybe a week —

but ultimately they were all released back to their homes in nature.

But then I got a tortoise. In the winter of 1999, I'd fallen hard for a Bell's hingeback tortoise after seeing a display of them at the pet store in the mall. In a hexagon pen in the middle of the store, filled with sawdust chips and a miniature wooden house, a dozen desert tortoises casually plodded, frequently pushing into each other, like bumper cars toward the end of the ride when the mechanisms wind down. Turtles were cool, yeah, but tortoises — they were majestic, thoughtful, serious. For months I saved up my allowance ($60, a truly extraordinary sum for a middle schooler in 1999!) and brought one of the African tortoises home. Inspired by his old-man wrinkles, his seemingly wise demeanor, and the A section of the book *20,001 Names for Baby,* I named the tortoise Aristotle.

Perhaps Plato would have better suited him; Aristotle was definitely not content being confined to the cave. He wanted to leave and experience the light of the world for himself. Every day he spent hours clawing at the corner of his tank, his head pressed against the seam of the two perpendicular glass panels, his front legs and the sides of his shell mashing into them. He seemed to think that if he pushed hard enough, one day that glass corner would give out and he'd be free. He probably missed the grasslands of Africa. Or he wanted to find another tortoise to hang with. Or he was deranged. But I didn't care; I loved him—his weird wrinkled face, his little claws, his methodical clunking.

But the thing I loved most about Aristotle was his life span: Bell's hingeback tortoises can live anywhere from twenty-five to sixty years in captivity. Catch-and-release wild pets were one way to avoid pet death; an animal that would live almost as long as a human was another.

But, as Aristotle would prove, even animals purchased in a pet store can be temporary pets. To try to quell the tortoise's pathetic scraping against the terrarium walls, when the weather got warmer, I took him out for walks. Our house in Lexington had a fenced-in backyard, and I would spend hours on the deck, letting Aristotle roam, getting up every now and then to grab him when he started to dig at a hole under the fence. I'd pick him up and bring him back near the porch, where he'd start again, jetting through the grass in spurts, pausing to rest, slowly pushing his way through dead leaves and stems, zigzagging across the yard, determined. But as much ground as a tortoise can cover, a human is faster. If the human is paying attention, that is.

Just like Kiki, Aristotle came with me and my family to Fishers Island each summer. There wasn't a fence around the yard at our summer rental, just a huge, grassy sprawl. Aristotle loved it out there—must have been reminiscent of the savannah—and in the summers I spent most of my time reading on the deck while he wandered. This was our routine for the summers of 1999 and 2000. Then came summer 2001.

One morning in June, I was off at the small island library when my dad got frustrated with Aristotle's relentless clunking. Dad took him outside and let him walk in the grass while he drank another cup of coffee and read the newspaper. Everything was fine — Aristotle striding through the dried grass, my dad picking him up and bringing him back — until the phone rang. My dad went inside to answer it and got sucked into a conversation for several long minutes; when he went back out, Aristotle was nowhere to be found.

I returned from the library to find both my parents and all of our neighbors scouring the area. I figured out what had happened pretty quickly. Screaming and crying, I didn't even let my father explain. I ran to my room, slammed the door, and wrote a long, angry, tear-soaked journal entry.

After several days of leaving out bowls of lettuce and overturning every plant and shrub, I realized that Aristotle wasn't coming back. My grandmother called to comfort me:

"Oh, Elizabethy, animals shouldn't be kept in cages. Think of how happy Aristotle is now. He's probably swimming with his other turtle friends in the ocean as we speak!"

"Nunni," I said darkly, "he's a tropical tortoise. If he's in the ocean, he's dead."

But as cynical a front as I put on to my family, I did hold out a secret hope for Aristotle's return. It's not impossible for a lost tortoise to resurface. In 1982, the Almeida family, in Realengo, Brazil, lost track of their red-footed tortoise Manuela. They searched, to no avail, and eventually gave up, assuming that Manuela, who had free range to roam the house, had wandered off after some maintenance workers had left the door open. They lived near a forest and figured that Manuela had made a new life for herself there. Thirty years later, cleaning out the house after their father died, the grown children opened a box they found in a locked storage closet. Inside the box, there was an old record player and a red-footed tortoise. Manuela had survived three decades living in a box, eating termites. She inspired Joey Soloway, the creator of the television show *Transparent,* to write a tortoise into the show in her honor: Nacho was lost, thought to be dead, but actually lived in the air ducts, eating bugs, spying on the Pfefferman family for decades, only to be rediscovered at the end of the third season.

But Aristotle was an African tortoise living in New England. His odds were not good. Unlike with Flower, I didn't have a lot of hope that he was off happily having adventures without me. Still, I never knew for certain: no body to bury, no hollowed-out shell found in the grass. Aristotle simply vanished. There was nothing to confirm his death, no tactile object to hold on to in place of his absence. "People hunger for certainty," writes Pauline Boss in her book *Ambiguous Loss.* "Even sure knowledge of death is more welcome than continuation of doubt." Boss goes on to describe these types of ambiguous losses — loved ones lost in war or plane crashes, their remains never recovered; kidnapped children; elderly relatives fading into dementia or Alzheimer's. I would add an MIA tortoise to that list, or any runaway pet.

All I wanted was to know for certain whether or not Aristotle was coming back. Oscillating between hope and despair was draining, and I craved a physical object as some sort of concrete evidence of what had happened. Something to hold on to. There's a reason why cleansing or viewing a loved one's body before burial is such a common practice around the world — seeing the body can help along the process of grieving and acceptance. But even a box of ashes, an old worn collar, an empty L.L.Bean dog bed — having any sort of object can help a mourner understand that, yes, your animal friend really is dead and gone. And if you can't find an object on your own, you can always commission something to help you grieve and remember.

At this point in my research, I have seen pet memorial

objects of all kinds: a quilt made from T-shirts featuring photo transfers of a dead black Lab; a memorial mural on the Lower East Side of Manhattan, outside a holistic pet care store; a sun-faded flag hanging on a house in Braintree, Massachusetts, with a photo of an English bulldog and the words IN LOVING MEMORY underneath; a memorial bench in a park in Portland, Oregon; a stained-glass window featuring a portrait of a deceased sheltie; a hand-carved headstone made by an artist in Vermont; a basket knit from spun Himalayan kitten fur; a million possible custom portraits available from artists on Etsy.

None of these are exactly huggable, though. For that you need Cuddle Clones, a company that can make you a realistic stuffed animal of your dead pet in eight weeks. Jennifer Williams, founder of Cuddle Clones, first thought of the idea for her company in 2005, when she was napping next to her dog Rufus. He was a harlequin Great Dane with different-colored eyes and very distinctive spots, and Williams daydreamed about how fun it would be to have a stuffed-animal version of Rufus that looked just like him. She tucked the idea away and didn't think about it again for a while—until Rufus died. Then, once her big guy was gone, all Williams wanted was to be able to hug her dog again—and Cuddle Clones was born. She founded it in 2010 with her business partner, Adam Greene. There's a surprisingly large market of people who want a realistic stuffed-animal version of their living pet—people traveling for work, kids going away to college, servicemen and -women sent out on deployment, elderly folks moving into an assisted living facility that doesn't allow pets. But Williams told me on the phone that about 60 percent of their business is customers who have recently lost a pet. When they started the business a decade ago, they had sixteen employees in the workshop and produced about thirty Cuddle Clones per week. By 2016 they had forty-six employees and were making anywhere from two hundred to three hundred Cuddle Clones a week. "People want to hold something," Williams said.

It's true. And sometimes the thing we want to hold on to isn't just a likeness of our dead pet but part of the dead pet itself—just like I'd hoped to find Aristotle's shell. Williams has received requests for custom Cuddle Clones containing pouches to hold a bag of the pet's ashes. And she's not alone in the market. One artist in San Diego, Simone Pixley Weinstein, makes a "Mourning Pillow" that you can insert your pet's ashes into and hug. She came up with the idea after she suddenly lost her pug Nellie, who developed leukemia at age three. After Nellie's death, Simone, on a whim, cut open a teddy bear she had and put the bag of Nellie's ashes inside. "It was soft and warm, like my old dog," Simone explained. She would also write notes to Nellie and tuck them in the bear. "It made me more at ease during my mourning process," Simone told me. There are also artists who create gorgeous glass beads with bits of ash or fur swirled inside, and companies that press cremated remains into artificial diamonds so you can wear your beloved friend close to your heart.

Maybe, though, you want more than reimagined ashes. Enter taxidermy.

Now, I know that some readers just came to a screeching halt. For some people, taxidermy is too much, the uncanny valley — it looks alive but isn't alive, is real but not quite real. But hear me out.

Dave Madden puts it well: "Taxidermy is an art form that begins at the moment an animal dies," he writes in *The Authentic Animal.* He makes the point that death is an inescapable part of the taxidermy art form, even if the point of taxidermy is to make something dead look alive again: "To live eternally and to live again a thing must first be dead, and this is what taxidermy is. Death. The dead." So those who practice taxidermy, or seek it out to preserve their pet, must be comfortable with death in a way that many are not.

Taxidermy is far from a new trend embraced by pet people; turning pets into stuffed animals has been a thing for a long time. Just take Charles Dickens. He was obsessed with his cats. So much so that when his cat Bob died in 1862, Dickens had one of the cat's paws preserved and made into a letter opener. The paw was fitted with an ivory blade inscribed with C.D. IN MEMORY OF BOB 1862. In order to use the letter opener, Dickens would have had to grasp Bob's paw in a postmortem handshake, sending a little greeting to Bob on the other side.

And Dickens wasn't an exception. Taxidermy increased in popularity in the nineteenth century as taxidermists refined their skills. The invention of arsenic soap allowed for longer-lasting and more lifelike preservation of animal forms, and with that, the subjects expanded from hunting trophies to pets. It's one thing if a buck you shot and had preserved eventually decays; it's another if it's your best furry friend.

Taxidermy, in a way, is a rebirth — the animal you loved, in a new form, that can do new things. For Dickens in 1862, that meant turning his cat's paw into a useful desk implement. For Dutch artist Bart Jansen in 2012, it meant turning his beloved cat Orville into a taxidermy drone — fitting, since the feline was named after the famous aviator Orville Wright. Jansen wrote on the website for his business, Copter Company, "When Orville was killed by a car, I decided to pay tribute to his lost life by giving him a new one. Electronic life. How he loved birds." I have yet to hear of another individual who has turned a pet into a drone, but maybe that's just because what made sense for Orville doesn't make sense for any other cat. Remember: there is no one-size-fits-all in grieving. Orville has been preserved with his four legs sticking straight out in a starfish pose, the drone motor embedded in the dead cat's abdomen. Each one of Orville's paws is fitted with a propeller, and when the cat flies—and fly he does—with his wide glass eyes frozen in surprise, he looks straight out of a cartoon.

Drones aren't even as unusual as it gets. British artist David Shrigley spent a decade creating taxidermied cats and dogs standing on their hind legs, holding signs that read I'M DEAD. (Interestingly, Shrigley stopped creating these pieces once he got a puppy of his own.) And don't forget about the legendary Walter Potter, a Victorian-era taxidermist in rural England who was famous for his whimsical and strange taxidermy tableaus. In the small town of Bramber, he ran his taxidermy business—creating hunting trophies, preserving specimens for science—and next door to that he ran a small museum, where crowds flocked to see his displays of anthropomorphic taxidermy mounts: birds acting out nursery rhymes, frogs on a miniature playground, rats and squirrels playing card games, kittens having a wedding ceremony.

A lot of the creatures Potter preserved in his tableaus were "disposable" animals—rats killed by farmers, a surprise litter of drowned kittens. These animals were seen just as a commodity, a means to an end, a tool for the craft no different than thread or glue. But, at the same time,

Potter was also preserving beloved pets—animals with names, histories, stories, loved ones. One of Potter's very first bird mounts—created when he was nineteen, in 1854 —was his own pet canary. In his taxidermy museum, Potter displayed preservations of his pet cat (wearing a jaunty bowtie) and his friend's dog Spot (who apparently, before her death, survived being "buried alive for three weeks under heaps of straw at threshing time and later being shot when she was mistaken for a rabbit"). While I find all of Potter's work intriguing—I got to see the kitten wedding scene in person at the Morbid Anatomy Museum, in Brooklyn, in 2016—it's animals like Potter's canary and cat and the unkillable Spot that draw me in. These were animals with families and stories, and in preserving their bodies, Potter saved their memories alongside them.

"Taxidermy in all of its forms is a sculptural storytelling technique," writes Robert Marbury in his book *Taxidermy Art: A Rogue's Guide to the Work, the Culture, and How to Do It Yourself.* Marbury focuses on a group of contemporary artists who incorporate taxidermy mounts and skeletal forms into their own work. "Aspects of taxidermy artwork may make people uncomfortable," continues Marbury, "but the point is never to be ostentatious or deliberately offensive. Every piece is the artist's expression of his or her love and wonder of animals."

It's interesting, though, that despite this love for animals, many taxidermists are hesitant to preserve pets. (Potter was unusual in that regard.) Or maybe it's *because of* their love of animals—they get how intensely people love their pets. When I was in Paris in March 2019, I visited a couple of the city's fabled taxidermy stores—Design et Nature and Deyrolle—and saw very few pieces featuring domesticated animals. But there are some shops that will do it now, like Bischoff's Animals, in Los Angeles, and also some brave up-and-coming taxidermy pioneers—a majority of whom seem to be young women—who are taking on pet preservation. "My love is of animals and people—hearing their stories, especially when they don't have someone to talk to or that they feel they can trust . . . I like that the artwork I do can provide that space," explained Divya Anantharaman, the owner of Gotham Taxidermy, in Brooklyn. Lauren Kane-Lysak began her taxidermy business, Precious Creature, in Twentynine Palms, California, specifically wanting to preserve pets: "I love the idea of being able to memorialize, create something special," she told me.

Throughout our conversation, Kane-Lysak and I chatted like old friends, the way two people who love animals find it easy to connect. "With trophy taxidermy, the taxidermist opens a catalog of forms and you pick which one you want," she explained. At Precious Creature, every single piece she does involves a custom form. She thrives on the creativity and loves being able to help people in their time of need. She wants to help make the moment of death an exceptional one, a way of thinking inspired by Georgian and Victorian mourning practices.

People used to be much more open about their grief—the Victorians in particular regularly wore black clothing and donned memorial jewelry that often involved physical remains to outwardly express their mourning. Honestly, the Victorians were kind of obsessed with death, perhaps because it was all around them, given the less advanced state of medicine and sanitation at the time. Queen Victoria herself lost her husband, Prince Albert, when he was forty-two years old. She proceeded to spend the next forty years wearing black and making her servants lay out Albert's clothes every morning. Victoria's extreme mourning set a strong example for commoners of the era. People commissioned larger-than-life monuments in cemeteries, and big, elaborate funerals were seen as the ultimate sign of love. Victorian women were expected to wear all black for at least two years after the death of a family member; brooches and lockets made with the deceased's hair were all the rage. "Victorians braided hair into memorial pieces, because they saw it like a portal to the other side," Kane-Lysak explained. "The piece of anatomy was a direct line to heaven." Death was something to understand, to celebrate, even. "Cemeteries used to be parks," she told me. "People would have picnics there. There was wonder in death, curiosity."

Kane-Lysak seems to have that wonder and curiosity herself, but when it comes to her work, she understands that the creatures she's commissioned to preserve are part of an animal that was once — still is — deeply loved by a person. She encourages her clients to write a letter to their pet and add it, along with toys and flowers, into the dry ice cooler when they ship her their pet's body. Throughout the whole preservation, Kane-Lysak keeps in contact with her clients and texts them updates — she even sends photos of the work in progress if the client wants to see. And if a client lives in Southern California — her studio is just outside Joshua Tree National Park — she encourages them to bring the bodies of their pets to a special room in her home studio for a wake-like viewing before beginning the taxidermy process.

Kane-Lysak explained that having time with the physical body of a departed loved one — human or non-human — is extremely important for the grieving process. Sometimes people will call her right after their pet died, before they're even sure if taxidermy is what they want to do; they're just looking for help. "They know they don't want to leave their pet just yet," she explained. She encourages them to wrap the body and keep it in a freezer, maybe with flowers or favorite toys. "You can even take them out to talk to them, to say hello, every once and a while," she added. "It sounds weird, but it can really help that mourning process just to have a little extra time."

During our phone call, I was blown away by Kane-Lysak's compassion and care for her clients—both the grieving people and the departed pets—and could easily see why her work is in high demand. At the time we first talked, in March 2019, she was working on twenty-seven different animals, ranging from full taxidermy mounts to skull and skeleton cleanings to paw and coat preservations to a few simple cremations. She does it all, and she's worked on creatures ranging from a dwarf hamster named Daisy (her first pet taxidermy piece!) to a sixty-five-pound pit bull to scorpions, parakeets, canaries, crows, parrots, and quail to her own pet tarantula. Kane-Lysak also makes a point of offering payment plans for taxidermy pieces—she charged $5,000 for the sixty-five-pound pit bull, which apparently is low for taxidermy. She wants to make taxidermy accessible to anyone who would benefit from it. "The most rewarding part of my job is the gratitude from my clients," she told me. "It's a way to change a really, really sad situation into something beautiful, and that is really rewarding."

Divya Anantharaman, of Gotham Taxidermy, echoed that sentiment when I toured her Brooklyn studio. Anantharaman got into the practice while she was in fashion school: she used leather, feathers, bones, and skulls in her jewelry and wanted to understand how they were preserved. Then, on a cold winter hike, she came across a frozen dead squirrel and took it as a sign to try her hand at preservation. Now she works full-time as a taxidermist and has won several contests for her work. Her specialty is birds, and she makes a lot of gorgeous art pieces featuring winged creatures, but she began working with pets not long after she started doing taxidermy. (Her first pet commission was a rat.) The pet work definitely isn't her biggest moneymaker. In fact, she barely breaks even and sometimes takes a loss on her pet pieces — she spends more time on them, wanting to make sure they're absolutely right, and she doesn't charge people as much as maybe she should because she feels bad making money off people when they are grieving.

"People feel they have someone to talk to about wanting to preserve their pet," Anantharaman told me when I visited her studio. "They feel seen, and feeling seen is very valuable." Like Kane-Lysak, she offers a range of services — from traditional taxidermy mounts to skeleton and bone cleaning to partial preservations. Anantharaman will even do a whole display with preserved flowers — beautiful works of art in their own right. She also offers freeze-drying as an option — she doesn't do it herself in her studio but works with someone who does.

Both Kane-Lysak and Anantharaman usually preserve pets using traditional taxidermy technique—completely disassembling the animal, removing and disposing of the organs and bones, tanning the hide, and reassembling the skin and fur over an artificial form with glass eyes— but freeze-drying has become a popular alternative. With freeze-drying, the animal isn't taken apart in its entirety— the eyes are removed and replaced with glass fakes, the organs are removed and replaced with artificial fill, and then the body is injected with distilled water and embalming fluid. After that, the animal is manipulated into the desired pose, tacked to a piece of wood, and placed in a freeze-dryer for anywhere from a couple of weeks to a couple of months. In a freeze-dryer, the body is exposed to extremely cold temperatures (below zero degrees Fahrenheit) and vacuum pressure, which removes all the moisture from the animal's tissue, but at a rate slow enough that the cells retain their shape. A freeze-dried pet can look more like the living pet, because the animal hasn't been taken apart and reassembled. The downside is that freeze-dried forms are more prone to moisture and insect damage.

But freeze-drying is just the right thing for some people. Take Monica La Vita. When I met La Vita for coffee one winter afternoon in Somerville, Massachusetts, all I knew about her was that she was a mortician and that she'd preserved her Boston terrier. It didn't take long for me to find her in the coffee shop—pale skin, dark hair, lots of tattoos (not to stereotype). "I knew all along I would taxidermy him," La Vita told me, right away, about her dog Ace. (She technically had Ace freeze-dried and not taxidermied, but in our conversation we used the terms interchangeably.)

The dog had come into La Vita's life when she was fifteen, and she said that by the time she was sixteen or seventeen she'd already decided that taxidermy would be his final fate. "Having my dog's remains in a box felt weird," she shrugged and sipped her coffee. "I needed to see him every day." And I get it—Ace had, and still has in his preserved form, a distinctive look. By the time he died, at age eleven, he was missing his right eye after developing glaucoma, and he had a long, pink tongue that permanently hung out of his mouth. It took La Vita a while to find someone who would work on Ace, but she finally found a guy in California who would freeze-dry him. She packed Ace up and shipped him out. The freeze-drying process took nine months, and when Ace finally returned to La Vita, she cried happy tears. "Financially, it was the best idea I've ever had," she said.

La Vita appreciates that the Ace she got back from the freeze-dry guy is not the same Ace who was once alive. "If you are okay with having the animal around without their personality—no sniffing, no barking, just his shell—then I recommend taxidermy," she said. She likes seeing

Ace there—he lives in a glass case about the height of a small side table—and she takes him out once a month to pet him. The oil from her hands helps preserve him, and she enjoys having the chance to rub her hands on his fur again, to talk with him. "Really, I stand by my decision 110 percent," she insisted. I asked if she'd gotten any pushback. Her dad was not on board at first but has warmed to the idea; some of her friends initially had discomfort but ultimately got over it; her boyfriend thinks she's nuts; her hairless cat, who used to cuddle with Ace when he was alive, likes to hang out on or near the glass case; and La Vita's three-and-a-half-year-old son simply thinks of taxidermy Ace as one of his pets—he tells people that they have an "alive kitty and a dead puppy" at home.

When I asked La Vita about her advice for people in mourning—which, as someone who works in the funeral industry, she has plenty of experience with—she said simply: "Do whatever you need to do." Clearly, she took her own advice to heart.

I asked her if she plans to preserve her pets in the future. "I don't know," she said. "I don't see myself carrying around another preserved animal." That could get unwieldy—a whole army of preserved cats and dogs to move from apartment to house to nursing home. But she is thinking of preserving her cat's skull one day.

Taxidermy will never be for everyone. This is something

Kane-Lysak is really careful about: trying to educate people on the difference between a preserved cat and a real cat. It may seem obvious — one is dead, the other alive — but sometimes people don't quite realize what they're getting into. "People are really sheltered from death," she said, "and they almost expect a living, breathing pet back." Of course, no matter how good Kane-Lysak is at taxidermy, she can't bring your pet back to life. "Some things won't translate," she told me. "The soul is no longer there, and that is something we never will be able to replicate, no matter how good the eyes look or how perfect the pose. The very vital essence is missing." She has had a few cases with clients asking for nitpicky alterations of features, or some who have gotten cold feet and ghosted her, leaving her with their preserved dead pet forever. But she tries to let it slide; she understands that it's usually their grief speaking. "I would not want to deal with me grieving," she laughed. Still, though, she tries to make it as clear as possible to clients what taxidermy is all about, to avoid such situations. She explains taxidermy to potential customers as "preserving the house that housed the soul," and she has examples of taxidermied pets in her studio for people to see and touch. (The ones that the ghosts left behind.) If people can understand that, they generally won't be alarmed when they get back their taxidermied pet.

I spoke to Kane-Lysak again in 2021, to see how things

were going with her business during COVID. She said she'd hit a dry spell during the first few months, but since then she's had more people contacting her for preservations than ever before. Every day she gains more followers on Instagram, and one friend's younger nieces and nephews are encouraging her to get on TikTok. But it seems like she doesn't need it: "I'm at full capacity," she told me. "I'm having to refer people out." I had to admit I was surprised. Considering that so many people lost their jobs during the pandemic, splurging on a full taxidermy form of your dead dog seems like it would be the first thing to get cut from your list of spending priorities. (Though perhaps, if you got a COVID stimulus check and didn't really need it, you could finally get the taxidermied dog of your dreams.) "People are still spending money on their pets, and now they are spending extra time with them," she pointed out. "It almost makes parting with them even harder, so of course people are going to be looking for these kinds of services." Plus: "People are more openly talking about death all the time now," she said, almost the opposite of what she told me when we first spoke in 2019. "As a Western culture we are so closed off to death, but we've all been thinking about it all the time since last March." I asked if she thought we were returning to Victorian death culture. "Maybe," she said. "People are simplifying and looking inward to what's really important and really only investing their money into things that will spark joy."

Still, there are plenty of ways to preserve part of your pet's physicality without going for a whole preservation. Kane-Lysak often will taxidermy just part of a pet for a client—a tail, an ear—or clean and reassemble the skeleton. Many veterinary practices will make an impression of the animal's paw print before cremation, to return to the client along with the ashes. Kane-Lysak also offers nose casts of dogs and cats, which I had never heard of before but immediately loved the idea of. I wished I could have asked her to make a cast of Aristotle's scaly little nostrils back in 1999.

Arguably the most extreme way of preserving your pet's body, though, is to re-create it in the form of another living being—which is to say, clone it. Cloning has always been controversial. Anti-cloners feel it's unnatural, an attempt at playing God. They say the money spent on cloning would be better spent caring for an already living animal, and that the animal surrogates required to carry the future clone to term can't consent. There also aren't many laws and regulations regarding cloning, and the ethics of it are murky at best, especially when it comes to cloning or genetically manipulating primates or humans. When people speak of using cloning to edit out diseases from our DNA, it can quickly turn to a conversation about eugenics.

But even taking all that into account, there is indisputably a market for pet cloning. EGOT legend Barbra Streisand has two cloned pups, Miss Scarlet and Miss Violet, both replicas of her dog Samantha. "I was so devastated by the loss of my dear Samantha, after fourteen years together, that I just wanted to keep her with me in some way," Streisand wrote in an opinion piece for the *New York Times*. "It was easier to let Sammie go if I knew I could keep some part of her alive, something that came from her DNA." In the end, four puppies were yielded from the cloning process, though Streisand ended up with only two — the runt of the litter died before she could bring the puppies home, and since she'd already adopted two more pups while waiting to see if the cloning process would work, she ended up giving one of the clones to the daughter of a family friend.

If you're interested in pulling a Barbra, there are several companies that specialize in pet cloning now, like Sinogene, the company in Beijing that created China's first cat clone; Not You But You, the first dog-cloning company, which is a partnership between the American firm H BION and South Korea's Sooam Biotech Research Foundation; and ViaGen, the Texas-based animal-cloning company that Streisand used. ViaGen will clone any non-primate mammal: dogs, cats, sheep, goats, pigs, horses. I spoke with Codi Lamb, one of its client service representatives, about the work they do. Lamb, who'd worked at ViaGen for four years when I spoke to her in the winter of 2019, told me that she's the main point of contact for clients once they decide to go forward with the cloning process.

My first question was why someone would want to clone their pet. Lamb rattled off a list of reasons that I hadn't thought of: maybe you spayed or neutered your pet before realizing you wanted to continue the lineage; maybe your pet was a mutt with a unique look that would be impossible to re-create through breeding; maybe you just want to know that some of your pet's DNA is still alive somewhere. I was surprised to learn that most of the people who opt to preserve their pet's DNA through ViaGen don't ultimately go forward with the cloning process. "Just preserving the DNA is enough to give some people peace," she explained. (Also, the $50,000 price tag might hinder many people from going through with cloning.) Lamb pointed out, too, that while a cloned pet will have a lot of physical similarities to your previous animal, physicality isn't necessarily what made your pet the pet that it was.

I spoke to one of ViaGen's clients, John, and he told me he's "a little bit private" about what he did. Some of his family members know that he had his beloved dog Princess cloned, and others do not. John is a retired New York City policeman, who adopted Princess after someone turned her in as a stray at his precinct. Princess moved in with John in 2006 and the two bonded right away, and after he retired in 2008 they only became closer. John and Princess were so in love with each other that John's then girlfriend actually got a little jealous; the girlfriend didn't last, but Princess was with John until she died.

John first started thinking about cloning Princess in 2016, when she got sick with cancer. He'd seen a BuzzFeed video called "I Cloned My Dead Dog" and it got him thinking. He decided to preserve Princess's DNA, just in case. Then she died, in March 2017. John spiraled. "And here I am, a policeman! I've been through a lot," he said. He had another dog at the time, a rescue named BeeBee who'd been close to Princess, and John said that BeeBee picked up on his sadness. Both John and BeeBee spent a year moping around. Finally, almost twelve months to the day after Princess's death, he decided to pull the trigger.

"I remember the exact spot where I was sitting when I got that call," John told me. It was September 21, 2018; two days earlier, the surrogate had given birth to two Princess clones. Twins! John was overjoyed. The puppies arrived at LaGuardia Airport from Texas on November 19, and John named them Ariel and Jasmine—Disney princesses, in honor of Princess. They looked like mini versions of his old dog. John sent me photos and videos of Ariel and Jasmine and also photos and videos of Princess, and often it's impossible to distinguish who's who unless he tells me.

John hadn't known Princess as a puppy—she was about

two or three years old when he adopted her—so at first he wasn't sure exactly how Ariel and Jasmine measured up personality-wise, but when we spoke on the phone in August 2019, the puppies were eleven months old and, he said, were developing more and more of Princess's mannerisms every day. He told me that Ariel and Jasmine were doing everything the same—they spun around together, they barked in unison, and when John said, "Who's there? What's that?" they both would look up toward the window by the door in the same way Princess used to.

In the end, John spent $50,000 to get Ariel and Jasmine, something that a lot of people are shocked to hear, but the way he sees it, people splurge on expensive Mercedes and BMWs in their retirement years—why couldn't he spend that money on a clone of his Princess instead? "I'd prefer to have my angel back and drive an old car," he said. But John knows that some who may want to pursue DNA preservation or cloning simply can't afford it, and also, in general, cloning is not for everyone. "The whole circle-of-life thing, I understand that," he told me. "But I wanted a piece of her back. And I wanted to do it for her, too. I wanted Princess—I know it sounds strange—to feel that love and connection again."

5

Bettas & Burials

URING THE FALL OF 2006, the beginning of my
first year of college, I experienced many life mile-
stones, most notably: getting the first-ever pet I didn't have
to negotiate with my mom for. She was a purple betta—
sometimes called a Siamese fighting fish—who lived in a
small plastic tank on the top of my tall oak dresser in my
Wellesley dorm room with me and my two roommates.
Her name was Wanda.[*]

Wanda saw me through the fall of my first year, and
things with her were great: she was active, swishing around
her tank, an entertaining break from studying. There had
been tension in my freshman triple—we were three ex-

---

[*] Only years later would I realize the big fanned fins of the fish meant
the betta was actually a male, but gender is a construct anyway, right?

treme personalities with wildly different interests and hab-
its—but we had Wanda in common. An uneasy silence
could always be broken with a comment about the fish; the
betta brought us together.

Wanda lived through winter break, survived car jour-
neys to and from my parents' house during vacation,
and managed to see the first glimmers of spring. I'd even
started to think about where Wanda's tank would go in my
sophomore-year room. But then one day:

"Are fish supposed to look like this?"

It was the end of April. I announced the question to the
room, and my roommates appeared by my side, our faces
touching as we peered into the tank, so close our breath
fogged the plastic. We peered into the one-gallon tank, full
of neon pink rocks, a fake plant, a gray plastic castle, and
a sick-looking betta. Our beloved Wanda was not doing
well.

"She looks . . . swollen," one roommate said.

"Kind of puffy," said the other.

"Why are her scales sticking out like that?"

Wanda floated in her tank, barely bothering to move her
fins, ignoring the flakes of food I sprinkled on the surface
above her enlarged head. Her scales—normally a bright,
shiny purple—were muted and protruding, no longer lying flat against her skin.

My roommate Lee, who was studying, appropriately, both the premed sciences and marine biology, turned to her computer. After a few minutes, she had the diagnosis:

"Dropsy. It's definitely dropsy."

"What's that?" I asked.

"It's when the fish can't expel water anymore but keeps absorbing it. That's why she looks bloated: she's full of water—even her organs. Listen: 'When your fish resembles a pinecone, it's too late.'"

We glanced back at my dresser. Wanda looked like a spiky, violet pinecone.

"How does a fish get dropsy?" I asked, a sick feeling swelling inside of me. While all three of us treated Wanda as our communal pet, she was my fish and, therefore, my responsibility. If Wanda was sick, it meant that I'd screwed up somehow.

"It's when some sort of virus or infection gets under their scales and into their system." I would learn years later that this is also called Malawi bloat. Lee continued: "The website says it usually happens from using tap water instead of treated or bottled water."

"Oh."

Everyone went quiet. Lee looked at me, narrowing her eyes.

"Did you use tap water, E.B.?"

I thought of the night some weeks ago, feeling cheap

and lazy, sleepy from a couple of drinks with classmates, too tired to go down to the basement to grab a bottle of Poland Spring from the vending machine, deciding that the dorm tap water must be good enough for a fish.

No one said anything.

"So what do we do now? Do we just wait for her to die?" Lee sighed. "I guess."

A long week passed. I woke up every morning hoping to find Wanda floating on the surface, but every time she persisted in pathetically living, bobbing in the water, even more swollen and globular than the night before.

After seven days I said, "I can't take it anymore." I felt terrible every time I looked at her, and, worse, the poor betta was clearly suffering. It was time for Wanda to go.

Lee began her next phase of research: humane methods of fish euthanasia. We ruled out flushing, which was called "the coward's method" of killing a fish—waiting for water treatment plants to finish it off after many hours in plumbing, still alive and desperate. One site suggested beheading the fish with a sharp knife, which I didn't feel up for. We settled on suffocation by grain alcohol. I trudged up to the fourth floor, to ask two older friends about a large bottle of Poland Spring vodka they had in their room. When I explained what I needed it for, they followed me downstairs to the first floor. My roommates joined me, along with a friend who'd walked across campus for moral support. The six of us crowded into the room and I filled two cups: one full of water and a sickly betta, one full of Poland Spring vodka. (Oh, the irony.)

"Okay," I said. "I guess I have to do it, don't I?"

Everyone was quiet. I threw back a shot of the Poland Spring in solidarity—gagging as I picked up the betta-filled cup, slipping her into the burning, clear alcohol. All her dropsy-induced lethargy suddenly gone, Wanda flipped, frantically fighting; her will to live was back. The fish snapped like a flag in a hurricane, breaking the surface of the vodka with sharp splashes. She twisted side to side, her gills cutting the surface and her miniature mouth opening and closing in a perfect circle. One final shiver, and finally Wanda was still.

The six of us went out into the dorm courtyard, a balmy May night, and buried the limp, bloated betta in a hole that I dug in the newly defrosted ground with a spoon pilfered from the dining hall. We buried Wanda with the contents of her tank: the fake plant, some pink stones, and the plastic castle. We had a moment of silence. Someone poured out some vodka. I was sad that Wanda was gone, but I looked around at what she had left me with. She'd helped me find a group of friends who were down to hold a funeral for my pet fish.

Even though the magic of the memorial service would be dampened the next morning when Lee and I spotted a family of squirrels digging up Wanda's grave, I kept thinking about the ceremony we'd had for Wanda. Though I'd had plenty of fish funerals before, back then I was usually burying the fish alone. This was the first time I had been surrounded by a whole group of people who understood. They say that funerals aren't for the dead; they're for the living. That was certainly true at Wanda's funeral.

As an event, it was simple and impromptu, exactly what I needed in spring 2007, but other pet people are drawn to more lavish memorials for their animals. Take, for instance, the funeral that Mozart had for his pet starling. On May 27, 1784, Mozart purchased a small songbird at a market. He had his pet starling for about three years and became quite attached to it. Classical music lore states that he loved the bird because it learned to sing the motif from the composer's newest piano concerto; some of Mozart's later compositions were inspired, in turn, by the starling's song.

Naturally, then, when the starling died, on June 4, 1787, the composer gave the bird a funeral with as much pomp and ceremony as any human funeral of the time. He hadn't traveled to his own father's funeral in Salzburg two months prior, but on the day of the bird memorial, Mozart got all dressed up, and the assembled mourners were all "heavily veiled." They processed to the graveside, where they sat and listened to Mozart recite a poem he'd written in the starling's honor: "A little fool lies here / Whom I held dear— / A starling in the prime / Of his brief time." He even gave the bird a proper inscribed gravestone.

In her book *The Pug Who Bit Napoleon,* Mimi Matthews writes of a clergyman who had an elaborate funeral for his "obese, black and white female" cat in 1897, allowing her to lie in state in his drawing room in a "brass-bound oaken coffin, with inner linings of silk and wool," before taking a train to the North of England to have a private funeral ceremony for the cat. Just as Lauren Kane-Lysak, the taxidermist, had told me: Victorians did not discriminate when it came to who was worthy of a funeral. Or at least some of them didn't.

Matthews also writes in her book about the March 1894 edition of the *Cheltenham Chronicle,* which described an elderly Kensington woman's funeral for her seventeen-year-old cat Paul. I can immediately imagine the woman—in Victorian times, "elderly" would have meant in her forties, so Paul would have been her companion for almost half of her life. She found an undertaker who conducted the funeral "as if it had been the interment of a human person of some importance," the *Cheltenham* reporter wrote. "The [cat's] coffin, with a lovely wreath on it, was displayed in the undertaker's shop, where it was an object of intense interest and not a little amusement," the reporter concluded. While some Victorians took the time and effort to mourn for their pets, others clearly thought grief over a mere animal was a laughing matter.

I keep returning, as I research, to the idea that our love of pets and our need to grieve for them have remained constant for centuries—but so has the judgment that comes with it. So often, when I spoke with pet owners for this book, they shared painful stories of being told, while in the throes of unbelievable grief, that it was "just a cat" or "just a dog." In other words: *Get over it.* Even people who have pets themselves can be quick to judge someone else's grieving as over the top. I've said that grief over pets is a disenfranchised grief; it's a loss that we don't talk about as openly as, say, losing your parents or grandparents. Is that, then, what makes people, even other pet lovers, uncomfortable with those who mourn so freely and boldly?

Some of this discomfort must also come from the contradictory views that different religions have on whether or not animals have a soul, as humans do. During Victorian times, while there were people open to pet funerals, there were also vocal protesters of animals receiving any sort of Christian burial. The *Edinburgh Evening News* reported in September 1885 on an older woman who attempted to bury her cat Tom in a human cemetery but was met by a "crowd of youngsters who followed [and] became exceedingly noisy . . . hooting and yelling vociferously, crying that it was a shame and a disgrace to bury a cat like a Christian." Tom's coffin was eventually smashed, his body was removed, and the police were called to the scene, staying on duty "till a late hour in order to protect [the woman] from the violence of the crowd."

But as stringent religious orthodoxy has become less and less common in so much of the world, our attitudes toward pets have changed. In 1990, Pope John Paul II reversed course on centuries of Catholic dogma and said that animals do have souls. In his thinking, God created humans by breathing life into them, thus giving them souls, and various parts of the Bible state that animals have the breath of life, too. "The existence therefore of all living creatures depends on the living spirit/breath of God that not only creates but also sustains and renews the fact of the earth," the pope said. "The animals possess a soul, and men must love and feel solidarity with our smaller brethren."

Bishop Thomas Brown, of the Episcopal Diocese of Maine, told me that over his career so far he has performed four pet funerals—three dogs and one cat. I asked if this meant he thought animals had souls, and he said he wasn't exactly comfortable saying that—that he had performed the funeral more to help the grieving family than for the animal. "Dogs have souls and are soul-filled," Bishop Brown told me, "but the need for redemption seems absent for me." The way I understood the bishop, as he continued to explain his stance, was that animals are not soulless, in that they're not just objects, but they don't have the same kind of troubled, conflicted souls that humans have. Animals do not intentionally do things that are wrong or harmful. "Animals are never dishonest," Bishop Brown continued. "Animals are pure and vulnerable already. They need more protection than people."

Franciscan priest and author Richard Rohr writes in his book *The Universal Christ* about the death of his fifteen-year-old black Lab, Venus: "My dog Venus taught me more about 'real presence' over a fifteen-year period than any theological manual ever did . . . Venus taught me how to be present to people and let them be present to me through the way she always sought out and fully enjoyed my company for its own sake . . . She literally modeled for me how to be present to God and how God must be present to me." At a bare minimum, animals are also God's creatures, and we should honor them as such. The Koran states that animals are conscious of Allah and worship him, though in a way that humans cannot fully comprehend. Rabbi Balfour Brickner explains in Wallace Sife's *The Loss of a Pet* that Jews, for thousands of years, have believed in humanely treating all living things—animals should not be forced to shoulder burdens too heavy, and back in the day it was forbidden for a man to eat before he fed and tended to his animals—even if the rabbi specifically avoided the soul question. But much as Bishop Brown observed, animals like Venus can teach us how to be present, how to be good, regardless of whether they have humanlike souls.

Eastern thought is just as conflicted on the topic as the Abrahamic religions. On one end of the spectrum, there is the ancient Indian religion of Jainism, which prohibits followers from brushing aside spiderwebs, squashing insects, picking fruit from trees, and, of course, killing animals for food. The core belief of Jainism is that correct living comes from empathy with all living creatures. Hindus and Sikhs believe that all beings — human and nonhuman — have eternal souls that are reincarnated in different forms after death; the fluidity between species is why many followers of Hinduism and Sikhism are often vegetarians. Buddhist leaders, meanwhile, are often at odds as to whether or not pet souls experience rebirth in the same way that human souls do. Some reject the idea of any Buddhist traditions being used for pets, as some associate animals with monsters and demonic spirits: keeping their souls close is seen as risky. Others suggest dogs are reborn as dogs, cats are reborn as cats, and so on. Some people fear their pets returning as "powerful, threatening spiritual forces" after their death, especially if the animal died through an accident or by euthanasia; others cradle the urns of their pets' ashes, unconcerned about angering any animal spirits by disturbing their rest, because pets enjoyed being touched and stroked in life. And some Buddhist clerics feel un-comfortable making a strong assertion one way or another and — as Barbara Ambros, a scholar of East Asian religions, puts it in her book *Bones of Contention* — "leave the post-humous fate of pets and the rationale for the performance of the rituals up to the imaginations of the pet owners."

Looking specifically at Buddhism in Japan, though, it seems that nowadays most Japanese pet owners consider their animals family, and treat them as such in death. (Ambros points out that the term people in Japan use most of-ten to describe their pets is "our child.") Buddhist pet fu-nerals seem quite common at this point, and deceased pets are given the same honors as deceased people: artificial or real flowers in vases, an urn for the ashes, a ceramic con-tainer for water or tea or sake, favorite foods, a name plate, a picture set by the grave (*dobutsu no haka no shashin*) or a memorial tablet (*ihai*). You might find some favorite toys or a collar. A deceased pet can also receive a *kaimyo*, or posthumous Buddhist name. And many Japanese pet cem-eteries hold memorial services several times a year, where pet caretakers can purchase additional prayer tablets, flow-ers, and wreaths to honor their departed animals.

There's definitely a contingent of Japanese pet owners who just call the local sanitation department when their animal dies and have a garbage truck come pick up the de-ceased (which must be in a box clearly labeled, for exam-

ple, "cat body"). But even those who choose the unsenti-
mental garbage-truck option often place offerings of food
or flowers near the clearly labeled box, preserving some el-
ement of Buddhist tradition.

My then boyfriend (now husband) Richie and I went to
Japan in March 2017 to visit my college roommate Lee—
the same one who'd diagnosed Wanda with dropsy and
who had been living in Japan since 2012. Richie and I each
made a list of necessary destinations to visit—the bam-
boo forest in Kyoto, the ancient temples in Nara, views
of Mount Fuji, and Sekai Dobutsu Tomo no Kai, the pet
cemetery on the grounds of Jindaiji, the second-oldest
Buddhist temple in Tokyo. I, naturally, was the one who
insisted that Jindaiji be on our list of stops. Richie, being a
good sport, agreed.

It took over an hour, on two different trains, to get to
western Tokyo, where Jindaiji is located. When Richie and
I left the Chofu station to walk the thirty minutes to the
temple grounds, we realized we were traipsing through
the Tokyo suburbs: narrow stone and stucco houses, small
fenced yards, bicycles, scooters, laundry hanging out to dry
on a balcony.

We eventually found our way to the entrance of Jindaiji
and were greeted by a map marking all of the oldest structures on the grounds and making note of the many soba

noodle shops, one of Jindaiji's specialties. But no mention of a pet cemetery anywhere on the map. I huffed in frustration. Where was it? Richie suggested we wander; we'd find it eventually. The temple grounds were peaceful — moss-covered stone walkways, a rounded wooden bridge over a stream, carved lanterns. People stopped to burn incense or leave offerings at the wooden temple, with its swooping black tile roof. Birds chirped, koi splashed, a turtle sunned himself on a rock — but there was no sign of a pet cemetery. My heart sank. The smell of the buckwheat noodles from the stalls near the entrance of the temple grounds began to catch my attention; maybe it was time to give up and have lunch.

But then I spotted an older man slowly walking his West Highland white terrier up the hill. That gave me hope — I hadn't seen a pet at any of the other ancient temples that Richie and I had visited. On a hunch we followed him, and then I remembered that I'd read that in the center of the pet cemetery was a tall stone stupa. I looked up and to the right and saw the stone structure peeking out through the trees; Richie and I followed the path toward it. We rounded the corner, and then I saw it: rows and rows and rows of wooden votive plaques hanging in front of the stupa. These are called *ema*, and we had seen them at every temple we visited — but these *ema* had whiskers and noses, cartoon drawings of dogs and cats in Sharpie on the wood, printed with paw prints and hearts. We had found the pet cemetery.

Richie and I made our way into the courtyard, toward the stupa, which was surrounded by shelves of framed photos of dogs and cats, next to small urns of ashes and piles of offerings of tins of dog food, bags of catnip, tennis balls, stuffed squeaky mice, and flowers.

I walked the rows of stacked stone graves—each approximately a foot cubed, dark black granite, engraved in a light gray. The graves showed names and dates of beloved pets, often written in both Japanese and English. A photorealistic portrait of a smiling corgi jumped out at me, framed by the phrase FOREVER KEVIN. An elderly looking golden retriever named Joy, a profile of a rabbit, a Shiba Inu wearing a hoodie. Some of the graves had windows carved into them, and I peered through glass to see the urn, photograph, or whatever other treasured objects were encased inside. Flowers in metal vases decorated the outside of each grave, along with candles. I listened to the birds and the chanting of monks in the distance, taking in the incense and sunshine, feeling calm. This was different from any of the pet cemeteries I'd been to in the United States or Europe, but also similar in so many ways. The love people felt for their pets was palpable and cross-cultural.

I worked my way out from the middle of the stone cub-

bies, stopping to read when I could, admiring the portraits. I realized when I reached the last row of stone graves
that the pet memorials continued inside the building surrounding the pet cemetery. The semicircular building
was a mausoleum, with four hallways lined with floor-to-
ceiling wooden shelves on each side, divided into hundreds
of cubbies containing photographs, flowers, urns, toys, and
food for dead pets.

I walked in and started making my way methodically
through each of the hallways, taking in the photos of dogs,
cats, hamsters, ferrets, gerbils, rabbits, chipmunks (chipmunks!), and even a pair of chickens. Richie hung back,
opting to stay outside—anything involving pet death
makes him emotional; his eyes were wet and he was already having a hard enough time looking at all the graves
outside, let alone inside. I tried to look at every shelf. I was
so distracted trying to take it all in that I didn't notice at
first that the doors leading out to the courtyard, which previously had been propped open, were being closed, one by
one. When I finally did notice, I panicked—was it closing
time? Was I about to be trapped in a Japanese pet mausoleum? I peered out the window on one of the closed doors
and went to test the handle—it wasn't locked. I breathed
a sigh of relief.

But as I looked through the glass window in the door, I
saw a procession of three monks—two in gray robes, one

in blue—enter the courtyard surrounding the stupa and the graves, chanting as they walked up to a large altar, under a white tent at the base of the stupa. I hadn't looked carefully at the altar when I first came in, distracted by the individual graves, but now I looked closely and saw the big bouquets of flowers, the piles of cans of dog and cat food, and the line of chairs facing the altar. The monks reached the front of the tent and continued to pray and chant, lighting more incense and candles, as a group of people sat and observed—many, it seemed, chanting and praying themselves. The people didn't seem to know each other—there was no chitchat, no friendly greetings, not even much acknowledgment between the individuals present. They all seemed to be engrossed in their own thoughts and reflection. One by one, each person went up to the altar, lit incense, and bowed three times, while the monks continued to chant, facing the altar of offerings. I stood at the door, watching out the window. I didn't dare leave the mausoleum. How could I, of all people, disrupt a pet memorial service? But also, where was Richie? That's when I saw him—surrounded by mourners, hanging to the back, his head bowed respectfully.

I would learn later that many pet cemeteries offer regular memorial services like this one, a yearly *segaki*, a Buddhist ceremony to "feed the hungry ghosts." *Segaki* are performed during Obon—the summer festival of the dead — and around the equinoxes. Richie and I were visiting in March, just days after the spring equinox. I couldn't have planned the timing better if I'd tried, and that day, peering through the glass window on the door, watching the monks chant and the pet caretakers light incense in honor of their dead pets, it felt like fate. I was overcome with emotion watching the ceremony. For a minute I wondered if perhaps Wanda or Kiki or Aristotle had guided me here.

The rituals felt somber and serious, and very old. As I'd learn later, many of the rituals practiced at Buddhist pet cemeteries are "invented tradition" — new practices based on old practices, and made to feel ancient and formal. Pets, in general, are fairly new to Japan. The first modern Japanese term for "pet" showed up in the early twentieth century, which is also when the country's first pet cemeteries were built — though archaeologists in Tokyo have discovered five tombstones for dogs and cats dating back to 1766. There are now hundreds of pet cemeteries in Japan, many of which are operated by Buddhist temples. And most of the ones that aren't on temple grounds are connected to Buddhist clerics. According to Ambros, most of the rituals performed at pet cemeteries were established in the 1930s and '40s, and only really became common in the 1970s and '80s. Now, on Shunbun no Hi, a Japanese national holiday for worshipping ancestors that falls on the vernal equinox each year, people visit the graves of their deceased pets as well as those of their deceased human ancestors.

The pet cemetery at Jindaiji is relatively new, too — at least compared with those I knew from the States. The Jindaiji pet cemetery was founded in 1962, and it's owned and operated by a private company, renting space from the temple. Ambros points out that many pet cemetery companies "use their presence on temple grounds as a means to promote themselves as quasi-religious institutions in the eyes of their customers. It's futile to try to figure out whether secular pet cemeteries are imitating Buddhist temples or Buddhist temples are imitating pet cemeteries." But I would learn that later.

I turned back into the narrow hallways inside the mausoleum, taking in more of the photos and offerings in the cubbies as I listened to the service outside. A photo of a Yorkie that looked a lot like my grandfather's dog Samantha peered back from one. A framed image of a hamster that looked a lot like Chuckie was surrounded by artificial pink flowers. A blond-white terrier with fuzzy triangle ears smiled at me from a sun-bleached image. I stared at the photo of the dog, the flowers to its left, the teacup to its right, and I took a moment to remember. Even though this place was not of my culture or my traditions, even though I couldn't understand the words of the Buddhist monks, even though I wasn't completely sure what it all meant, I felt grateful for those rituals, for that moment, because it gave me time. I thought back on all the animals I had known in my life, remembering the different things I had learned from them—love from Kiki, acceptance from Aristotle, responsibility from Wanda. The monks continued to chant for about thirty minutes while I stayed in the mausoleum, taking the time to remember.

Finally, when the monks processed out and the group dissolved, I found Richie, who looked thoroughly drained. He saw me and shook his head: "I can't believe that you, of all people, missed a Buddhist pet funeral." He sighed heavily and suggested we get some soba for lunch, and I told him I needed a minute to take a few more photos. Richie left the courtyard to wait for me on the path, and I turned back again to the outside memorials, pausing for a moment in the sunlight. When I first visited the Pine Ridge Pet Cemetery, outside Boston, I thought I got the point of pet cemeteries—you always know where your pet will be, you can always return to the same spot to sit with them, you always know where they were laid to rest, even if you move. When the veterinarian Dr. Samuel Johnson, who founded the Hartsdale Pet Cemetery, began burying pets in his apple orchard in Hartsdale, New York, he was doing it primarily for his clients who were Manhattan residents and had no access to a garden or yard to bury their animals. As Ambros puts it, a pet cemetery provides "spatial stability." All of that was true in the pet cemetery at Jin-daiji. But more than that, that day in the Tokyo suburbs, I was hit by something else — a feeling of community.

When Ambros was a foreign researcher in Tokyo in 1999, her parakeet, Homer, developed seizures and had to be eu-thanized. She was given two options: take Homer's body home to deal with herself or have him buried at a Bud-dhist pet cemetery. She chose the latter, out of "a sense of novelty and curiosity." When she eventually visited Hom-er's final resting place, Ambros was impressed by how well visited the pet cemetery seemed — full of fresh flowers, of-ferings of canned pet food, photographs, and other mem-orabilia. In *Bones of Contention,* she mentions that many of the Japanese citizens she interviewed were concerned about their pets being lonely in the afterlife: "Dogs that have never been separate from their human companion during their lifetime wouldn't be able to bear being buried in the mountains. They'd be lonely in such an unfamiliar place." Surrounded by dozens and dozens of other departed pets, Ambros felt this herself: "Homer is not likely to feel lonely."

So many human cemeteries feel cold and isolated, aban-doned, decaying, but that day in Jindaiji, in a warm patch of sunlight, surrounded by flowers and incense, affection-ate messages written by pet caretakers to their dearly be-loved pets, I could not imagine a less lonely place — for both the dead animals and their alive people. A community of humans who gather and mourn together several times a year, a community of animal spirits snuggled together in stacked cubbies — the living and the dead, together in love and companionship.

Stallions & Stardom

JUNE 4, 2008, was one of those rainy, bleak New England spring days. But the freezing downpour didn't matter—it could have been snowing for all I cared —because June 4, 2008, was a big day. I was finally going to the track with my grandfather, Puppy. For my entire life and then some, Puppy had frequented East Boston's Suffolk Downs horse racing track during afternoon breaks from running his insurance office in Somerville. He didn't go to the track for the thrill of gambling; he went because he's obsessed with horses. He memorizes statistics of famous equines, devours books about them. He reads the *Daily Racing Form* every day. He saw the movies *Seabiscuit* and *Secretariat* on their opening nights. He could talk about American Pharoah winning the Triple Crown all day. Puppy first fell in love with horses as a little boy, growing up next door to a man named Paul who had two horses at his house in Somerville. "One was a palomino and one was a retired racehorse who was blind in one eye," he explained. "One day when I was very small, Paul picked me up and placed me on the back of the palomino and let me ride around his backyard and just —" Puppy's eyes got wide and bright as he remembered the feeling of being up on that horse, his amazement at the majesty of the animal. "Just wow." He's been hooked ever since.

As a kid, I was desperate to go to Suffolk Downs with him, but Puppy never let me tag along. He'd make up some excuse about how the track was full of "degenerates" and change the subject. I pleaded with him for decades until finally, right after my sophomore year of college, he took me and my mother with him one rainy day in June.

The Downs was less glamorous than I had anticipated. The place reeked of decades-stale cigarette smoke, and the wall-to-wall carpet was dusty and worn to the floor in places. (Mom started sneezing as soon as she walked inside — shocker.) When Suffolk Downs stopped live horse racing six years later and then, in 2017, permanently closed — the property sold to a developer — I wasn't surprised. The place had looked on the verge of shutdown in 2008. But once the horses started running, I saw the appeal. I had never seen horses run a race in real life before. On television all you can see is miniature versions of their bodies, each one topped by a small, brightly colored jockey, as they run the laps. The screen separates you from really feeling the action. But at the track, the horses are so much closer. You can see their tongues hanging out, wild eyes, muscles flexing as they hurtle by. You can hear the pounding of their hooves. Feel the rush of wind as they swoop by. You can tell how hard they are working, and how badly the horses, not just the jockeys, seem to want to win. Mom won $10.40 when a horse named Sweet Jazz placed third, and then another $7.00 on a horse named Dinner Backstage. Puppy and I joked that we'd turned her into a horse-betting junkie.

Then came the third race. Puppy and I bet on the number one horse, Sentimental Lisa, and cheered as she won. But our celebration was short-lived—seconds after Sentimental Lisa's victory, the number three horse, Farouche, came barreling into the finish line, took a bad step, and fell. Suffolk Downs, usually so loud and boisterous, full of cigarettes and jokes and drinks, went quiet. Stable hands brought out a freestanding white screen and propped it up between the horse and the grandstand, to block the view. A veterinarian joined Farouche behind the white screen. After a few minutes, a truck drove onto the track to haul away the body.

"Damn, damn, damn," Puppy said, shaking his head, near tears. "The one thing I didn't want to happen and it happened right in front of us. Right in front of us. That's

why I never wanted to take you. Damn, damn, damn."
Mom kept up an overly cheerful appearance as we attempted to restore the afternoon. We placed bets on the
fourth race, but right before it was supposed to go off, they
canceled it and the other five races scheduled for the day.
With the wet track conditions, they didn't want to risk any
more horses getting injured.* We left soon after. I was quiet
for the rest of the afternoon. I didn't know Farouche personally, of course, but that day she felt like my pet. I was
sure, of course, that Farouche's owners were feeling the
horse's death far more than I was, but still, for the time I
was at Suffolk Downs, it felt like that particular horse had
belonged to all of us.

Horses, more so than dogs or cats or other pets, often
belong—literally and figuratively—to many people. Famous racehorses are divided into shares and sold for people to invest in them, like they would in a company, but
also there's the simple fact that in the twenty-five years or
so of a horse's life, it gets to know a lot of people. First
there are breeders, who know the horse as a newborn
filly or foal. Then there are the owners, who purchase the
young horse from the breeders, assuming the breeders

---

* Years later I would learn that apparently Farouche died of a heart
attack right after crossing the wire, and that the track conditions didn't
have anything to do with her death.

don't keep the horse for themselves. If the horse is going to race, there is a whole slew of additional people: trainers, stable hands, grooms, veterinarians, jockeys, additional partial owners. And after the horse retires, she or he may go on to have a second career as a broodmare or a stud, a show horse, a jumper, a fox hunter, a trail rider, or someone's pet. Dozens—even hundreds—of people may get to know and become attached to a horse over the course of its life. And if we're talking about a famous horse, then there are also the fans.

Man o' War was born on March 29, 1917, and he quickly rose to fame as one of the most successful racehorses of all time. Of the twenty-one races in his career, Man o' War finished first in all but one—the August 1919 Sanford Memorial Stakes race, where he was beaten by the appropriately named Upset. Even with this one stain on his record, no one could deny that Man o' War was a champion, and people were obsessed. There were commemorative postcards and photos, limited-edition Christmas ornaments and clocks, embossed bars of silver and drinking glasses, lapel pins and notecards, all featuring the stallion. In every race Man o' War ran, he was the favorite, and three times in his career he had odds of 1 to 100. He was so adored that his birthday parties were broadcast on local radio—a photo from one shows Man o' War standing smugly behind not just one but two birthday cakes. Man o'

War's popularity didn't end once his racing career was over, either—during his retirement years, an estimated three million people came to visit "Big Red" at Faraway Farm, in Lexington, Kentucky.

But then, on November 1, 1947, at thirty years old, Man o' War died of a heart attack. It took thirteen men to lift the thirteen-hundred-pound horse from his stall at Faraway. His body was preserved, which was thought to be the first instance of a horse embalming. The average human body needs two bottles of the formaldehyde mixture to do the job; Man o' War required twenty-three. The champion was laid to rest in a casket that was six by nine and a half by three and a half feet and lined with silks in yellow and black, the colors of his owner, Samuel D. Riddle. Man o' War lay in state in the center aisle of the barn at Faraway Farm, watched over by his two most successful progeny, War Admiral and War Relic.

On November 4, 1947, racetracks all across the United States held a moment of silence at 3:00 p.m., coinciding with Man o' War's funeral. School was canceled in Lexington that day so children and adults alike could pay their respects, and more than two thousand people were in attendance as Man o' War was laid to rest. The memorial service was broadcast on NBC Radio and featured nine eulogies.

Initially, Man o' War was buried at Faraway Farm, and people made pilgrimages to his grave every year, but in

1976 he was exhumed, moved six miles across Lexington to the newly built Kentucky Horse Park, and reburied under a life-size bronze statue of his likeness. Thousands of people still visit Man o' War's grave every year, more than a hundred years after his birth.

Puppy and I were two of those visitors in June 2016, when we went on a trip to Lexington. Visiting the horse capital of the world was our Suffolk Downs trip on steroids. Puppy had always wanted to see horse racing country — it only seemed right, given his lifelong love of equines — and I had my own research to do. For, while my grandfather was going to Kentucky to see live horses, I was going to see dead ones.

We hired a tour guide from Thoroughbred Heritage Horse Farms Tours. His name was John, and he was a part-time tour guide and a part-time Presbyterian pastor. (At one point during our tour, John casually mentioned that he had officiated a funeral at the Kentucky Horse Park for a group of horses that had died after their water supply got poisoned. "I used the same script I use for human funerals," he said, "but then just threw in some Bible passages about horses — like how Jesus will come back on a horse, the four horses of the Apocalypse, and that part at the end of the Book of Job.") John picked us up outside the hotel in a van the first morning, and we headed out of the city. I'd told him that I wanted to see the final resting places of some of North America's most famous animals, and he didn't disappoint. Our first stop was Hill 'n' Dale Farm.

"Guess who's resting here?" John asked as we made our way down the farm's driveway. He gave several clues, horse racing trivia that was beyond my scope of knowledge: *His sire was Bold Reasoning. His dam was My Charmer. He won the Triple Crown in 1977. He was the only Triple Crown winner to be undefeated.* Puppy got it right away: "Seattle Slew!"

The driveway ended and John stopped the van at a green island in the middle of the asphalt and brick. A bronze horse, about two feet high, mounted on a pedestal also about two feet high, stood watch over a dirt bed covered with ivy. John explained that on big race days, the statue of Seattle Slew is dressed up with flowers. The grave was surrounded by four beech trees, and in the outer ring of the grassy spot, on the other side of the driveway, were the graves of several other horses that had been the pride and joy of Hill 'n' Dale Farm—Teeming, Madcap Escapade, Daijin, Theatrical, Mutakddim. The trees filtered the sunlight, casting a soft glow on the place. Everything pulsed with bright green, warm and alive and peaceful—the ideal resting place for a champion.

Seattle Slew's grave was our first of the day, but far from our last. After Hill 'n' Dale, John took us to Old Friends, a retirement farm for thoroughbreds, founded by former *Boston Globe* film critic Michael Blowen after a career change.

Blowen was inspired to start Old Friends after the death of Ferdinand, the winner of the 1986 Kentucky Derby and the 1987 Breeder's Cup Classic and recipient of the 1987 Eclipse Award for Horse of the Year. After he retired from racing, Ferdinand was sold as a stud to a breeding farm in Japan in 1994. But when he got up in his years and wasn't quite the stud he used to be — if you know what I mean — the farm sent Ferdinand to the slaughterhouse without notifying his former owners to see if they wanted him back. As horse dealer Yoshikazu Watanabe explained, "Ferdinand was disposed of during last year. He was getting old and was in some discomfort." The phrase "disposed of" jumps out at me; when most people talk about a beloved animal dying, they use phrases like "put down," "laid to rest," "put to sleep," even "let go." "Disposed of" is harsher, blunt, the way you talk about a resource you've used up and are done with, not an animal with feelings and a personality, not a champion racer that people have loved. There were even rumors that after Ferdinand was "disposed of," his body was turned into pet food. This caused outrage in the horse world, and people began adding buyback clauses in their thoroughbred contracts, stating that if the new owner no longer wants the horse, they have to ask the previous owner if they want them back before "disposing of" them.

But over the course of our day visiting horse graves, I learned from John that dead equines becoming pet food isn't all that unusual. The bodies of horses are dealt with in several different ways, and not many get pomp and circumstance. Embalming is saved for the most elite of the elite—horses like Man o' War. For other famous horses, like Seattle Slew, their bodies are buried whole and/or in a distinctive place. Barbaro was buried at Churchill Downs after he shattered his two front legs in the 2006 Preakness race. Go for Wand was buried in the Saratoga Race Course infield after suffering a fatal injury in the 1990 Breeders' Cup Distaff. Other successful horses, well loved but maybe not super famous, aren't buried whole—the tradition is to remove and bury only the thoroughbred's head, heart, and hooves: the head for the horse's brain, the heart for the horse's life spirit, and the hooves for the horse's athleticism. The rest of the body is then cremated or sent to a rendering plant— the places that chop up animal bodies and prepare them for other uses, like turning them into grease, oil, fat, tallow, soap, gelatin, or glue (à la Boxer in *Animal Farm*). Sometimes parts of the horse are preserved and put on display instead of buried: Electioneer, Leland Stanford's prize-winning racehorse, has his ears, scalp, and one hoof on view at the Iris & B. Gerald Cantor Center for Visual Arts, at Stanford University. And some horses don't even get that honor—their entire body is simply sent off to the factory.

As I listened to John explain these different processes—in particular, when he told me that the best strategy for burying a horse whole is to dig the grave when the horse is old and sick, lead the (still alive) horse over to the grave, and then euthanize it grave-side so its (still warm) body falls into the pre-dug hole — I felt all kinds of confusion. Who gets to decide which horses are worthy of what kind of burial? Who decides what kinds of animals are worthy of a burial at all?

These questions nagged at me as John showed me the rest of the horse graves: the dozens and dozens at Old Friends, the four at Walmac Farm (Nureyev, Miswaki, Alleged, and Risen Star), the two dozen horse (and one dog!) graves at Magdalena Farm (a working horse farm), and the ring of eighteen headstones at the Hamburg Place Horse Cemetery (in a grassy patch behind the parking lot of a Walmart). The graves varied in nature — some, like the ones at Walmac, were nestled in peaceful groves of trees like Seattle Slew's. Others — like the ones at Magdalena, pushed into a corner behind the alive horses' paddocks — seemed created out of necessity: a working horse farm is going to end up with dead horses. Old Friends Farm seemed to take particular care with its horse graves, but it is specifically a retirement home for old horses — dealing with dead horses is part of daily business. And it's not just a matter of who gets buried, but who gets a funeral. Every Memorial Day the staff at Old Friends has a ceremony honoring all the horses that died in the past year.

While I mulled over the question of which animals are worthy of a funeral, and what kind of funeral, I began to think about the financial stakes involved with racehorses. Was that why people made such a big deal when a race-horse died? They wanted to pay tribute to a great money-maker? Take Man o' War — every time the horse ran, people bet on the stallion, so there was a financial gain to be had every time he won a race. And as thoroughbreds, these horses cost their people thousands and even millions of dollars. They have bigger life insurance policies than most humans. But I doubted that the money was the main rea-son to have memorial tributes to racehorses — there is also an emotional investment. How else to explain all these horse graves, often decorated with flowers, flags, notes? Perhaps the more formal and elaborate the burial, the more beloved was the horse.

I tested this theory on the second day of our tour, when we visited Claiborne Farm. Ever since Puppy and I had started planning our trip to Kentucky, I'd had my heart set on trying to visit Claiborne, because this is where the big guy, the ultimate Triple Crown champion, the racehorse to end all racehorses is buried: Secretariat.

Secretariat was a god. The thoroughbred came onto the racing scene during a time when, according to his owner, Penny Chenery, "the country was in a blue mood." Secre-tariat's racing career spanned sixteen months in 1972 and

1973, through Watergate and the Vietnam War, and he lifted the spirits of the entire country. He was best known for his astonishing win at the 1973 Belmont, where he ran the mile-and-a-half track in two minutes and twenty-four seconds, two seconds faster than any other Belmont winner's time. With that race he clinched the Triple Crown, the first horse to win it since 1948. Watching the video footage of Secretariat's Belmont win gives me chills. Every time I see it, I hold my breath as I watch him surge ahead; the way he runs, with such power and ease — it's as if you're watching the divine.

And people loved him for it. When Secretariat retired from racing and returned to Claiborne to stud, the farmhands had to build an extra-tall fence around his paddock to block him from the view of mobs of fans. As he got older, Secretariat developed laminitis, a degenerative disease of the tissue in the hooves, which causes terrible pain for the horse and is usually incurable. As a result, in 1989, when he was nineteen, Secretariat was euthanized via lethal injection. He was the second known horse to be embalmed, but unlike his famed predecessor Man o' War, he had a small, private funeral. He was buried at Claiborne, near his sire, Bold Ruler, and his grandsire, Nasrullah, and the custom-built coffin was lowered into the ground with a crane while fans around the country were left on their own to mourn.

I asked Puppy if he remembered where he was when Secretariat died. I wondered if for my grandfather the famous racehorse's death was akin to the day Kennedy was shot. "Oh, pal, I don't know," he said. "When did he die? The eighties? I mean, I was running two businesses at the time and you were a baby and . . ." Puppy trailed off and looked into the distance, and then I noticed that his eyes had become a little wet. "It was his hooves, wasn't it? They had to put him down because of his hooves." Even if you never met the animal, even if you weren't present for his death, the feelings, the emotions, the weight of the loss — they all stay with you.

Visitors are more than welcome to come visit Claiborne and pay their respects to Secretariat at his grave, and, in droves, they do. John, Puppy, and I joined a tour of Claiborne with about thirty other people, led by a man named Rodeo, one of Claiborne's grooms. Rodeo seemed like a southern tough guy — lots of tattoos, a no-nonsense attitude — and yet he was clearly emotional talking about one of the horses he'd cared for who'd passed away a few months before our visit to Claiborne. "You take care of the same stallions every day," he said. "You get attached. And the horses get attached to the grooms, too." Rodeo told the tour about the time he went on vacation and another groom had to care for his stallions for a couple of weeks. When Rodeo returned to Claiborne, before he even got a chance to come around to the stables and dole out peppermints (the horses' favorite treat), the stallions could hear his voice. They began to whinny and jump at the stable doors, wild with excitement that their friend was back. Now Rodeo cares for a stallion named Data Link. Upon hearing his voice as he led the tour, Data Link stuck his head over the stable door, looking for a peppermint. He didn't seem all that different from a dog hearing her person's car in the driveway.

As we walked the farm, I asked Rodeo where the legend was buried, and he gestured to an understated small cemetery by the entrance. I had missed it the first time around —a little gated yard trimmed with hedges and a low fence, tucked behind a one-room brick house that serves as the farm office and bathroom. A wrought-iron gate flanked by two rooster statues marked the entrance to the cemetery. ("Be sure to pet the roosters," John whispered. "They're good luck.") Rodeo explained that this cemetery was full; they aren't adding new horses to the lot, but they have a much larger cemetery out in the back of Claiborne where the more recently deceased horses are buried. But still, I had been expecting a Man o' War–style tribute to the legend Secretariat—a larger-than-life monument or at least a small statue like the one for Seattle Slew. Instead, all the headstones in the cemetery were the same size and shape— none of them fancier than the others. It took me a while to find his, which read simply, SECRETARIAT 1970–1989. So much for my theory that the more famous the horse, the more elaborate the burial. But there was something beautiful in that simplicity. Lichen and moss covered the headstone, and clover flowered in the grass in front of it. The only thing that distinguished Secretariat's grave from the rest was a single American flag pushed into the soil in front of the headstone, just like they do in human cemeteries for veterans. Secretariat, the American hero.

There are a lot of different ways specific animals can become widely beloved by an adoring public. Search and rescue dogs, like the ones that worked on 9/11, and Frida, who saved twelve people's lives after the 2017 earthquake in Mexico, often receive medals and monuments in their honor. Some zoo animals develop huge followings, like the pandas at the National Zoo, who have been visited or watched on the zoo's Giant Panda Cam by millions of people. A rare great black hawk that flew off course and landed in Portland, Maine, attracted a cult following—songs were written in the bird's honor and eventually residents paid to have a statue of the bird erected after he succumbed to frostbite. And on a local scale, a police officer's K9 partner can become a beloved part of a community.

"Normal people leave their pets at home," Officer Mike D'Aresta said when I visited him at the Middletown, Connecticut, police station. "But we bring ours to work."

I laughed when D'Aresta said this, but I knew that the real joke here is that K9s aren't just pets—they're coworkers, colleagues, and sometimes lifesavers. Dogs have been used by law enforcement officers for more than a century to track escaped prisoners, wanted fugitives, and missing persons and to help locate explosives, drugs, and cadavers.

K9s are trained to be essential partners to their human police officers, and of course, like everything involving the police, they're not without controversy. Many animal rights activists disapprove of any animals being forced to do work they can't consent to—from racehorses to K9s. But also, if the dog's human handler is overly aggressive, racist, or violent, this can pass down to the dog in horrific ways: police dogs have been used to threaten civil rights and Black Lives Matter protesters, attack suspects who already have their hands up, and bite and hold on to apprehended individuals. "Innocent until proven guilty" doesn't really feel like it applies when a German shepherd has a death grip on your arm. Dogs were also regularly used by the Nazis to uncover hidden Jewish families, and more recently dogs have been used to sniff out migrants trying to cross the US border. Police K9 units, or at least what they are used for, don't exactly have the best reputation. There are plenty of unnecessary, militarized tools that police use in their jobs, and seeing what K9s can do, and knowing the decades of fear that enforcement dogs have instilled in marginalized communities, I did wonder, going into my conversation with D'Aresta, if there was a clear purpose to the dogs' presence on the force. Was intimidation the main factor? If I am against police officers having military-grade weapons, should I be against their having dogs?

But while a K9's teeth are valuable to the police, apparently the reason for keeping dogs on the force all these years comes down to the nose. A dog's sense of smell is estimated to be 10,000 to 100,000 times stronger than a human's, and nothing people have made comes close to replicating it. Scientists have had some luck with an "artificial nose" in a sterile lab setting, but out in the real world, with so many smells to keep track of, a real live Lab can do much better. Dogs have shown themselves to be ten times more sensitive to smells than even the best-performing detectors, and in one particular study, human-made detectors found only half of the buried explosive devices, while dogs found 80 percent. Dogs can, quite literally, save their handlers' lives.

So it's no wonder the bond between officer and dog is so strong. D'Aresta's boss, Sergeant Doug Clark, once had a K9 partner named Niko. "My wife called Niko 'wifey,'" Clark told me. "Niko was my work wife." When police dogs get too old to work anymore, usually they retire and become pets, just like guide dogs or other service animals. And just like guide dogs or other service animals, some retired K9s have a really tough time adjusting; seeing their person head off to work every day without them after they've been together 24/7 for close to a decade is a big change. But Clark told me that when Niko retired, he had a harder time with the adjustment than the dog did; Niko quickly got used to hanging out at home and getting fed snacks by Clark's wife.

But Niko wasn't just loved by Clark and his family — Niko was a hometown celebrity. When he died, the local paper, the Middletown *Patch*, ran an obituary about Niko, describing him as a K9 who "put it on the line every day." For seven years, Niko was by Clark's side; he survived being shot at, being choked. He and Clark even worked together to track down a fugitive on the FBI's most-wanted list.

And there are so many more like Niko. D'Aresta's K9 partner, Hunter, became more than a local hero. D'Aresta explained that in July 2017, Hunter was still working hard, chasing suspects, investigating crime scenes with his nose, and doing everything in the K9 job description. He'd even gotten a physical earlier in the month and received a clean bill of health. But toward the end of July, Hunter stopped eating. He still wanted to work, but something was off. D'Aresta took him to the vet and, after a lot of tests, Hunter was diagnosed with an aggressive form of liver cancer. D'Aresta had a couple of hours to make the decision, and he made the tough call to euthanize. The news spread, and suddenly, a few hours later, everyone had assembled—officers on duty, officers off duty, D'Aresta's ex-wife, his daughter and son, one of his best friends from the neighboring town's police department, even some of his former girlfriends. Everyone who knew and loved Hunter was there, and they all lined up. D'Aresta picked up Hunter one last time and carried him through the parallel lines of friends, family, and colleagues; they saluted. In the photo the Middletown Police Department posted on its Facebook page, D'Aresta has his face buried in the black cape of fur on Hunter's back. You can tell he's crying.

But that was just the beginning. The Facebook photo of D'Aresta carrying Hunter went viral, and thousands of people saw and responded to the image. Comments, likes, reposts. D'Aresta received messages, phone calls, painted portraits of Hunter; a man in Maine made a beautiful engraved wood portrait of the K9; someone sent a music box with a German shepherd on it. The Middletown midnight shift officers commissioned a painting of Mike and Hunter and also signed a big photo of the dog and the officer together. "It helped me to mourn," D'Aresta said.

So often people's relationships with their pets are a tiny, closed circuit. No one at your office knows, say, the ritual you and your dog have when you come through the door at night singing a show tune with your dog's name in the lyrics as your pup spins and dances. Maybe only your family and your closest friends know how you spend every Sunday morning lying in your bed with your cat on your chest as you slowly sip your coffee. Pets see our most private, personal selves—but that means that our fellow humans often have no idea of the intensity of our relationships, just how much these animals are involved in our lives, so when they die, people may be surprised at the depth of our grief. Famous animals—and now we have more famous animals than ever, because of the internet—have long been the exception. Thanks to races and local news reports and zoo livestreams, some lucky creatures can find a cult following of people who love them almost as much as their owners or caretakers. And that's lucky for those owners or caretakers—they know more than anyone that they are not alone in their grief when that animal dies. Just think of the outpouring of feelings online every time an Instagram pet celebrity dies. Abby Ohlheiser wrote in the *Washington Post*, in the wake of the death of Lil Bub (@iamlilbub), "Watching the lives of other people's pets has become a part of the Internet experience, and now so has mourning their deaths."

But of course, people knew and loved celebrity animals long before Instagram—just look at how many people turned out for Man o' War's funeral in the 1940s—and sometimes nothing quite beats a real live connection. Before Puppy and I left Kentucky, driving down Man o' War

Boulevard to the Lexington airport—yes, the city of Lexington named its main road after its favorite dead racehorse—we had one last stop to see a particular live horse. John, our tour guide, drove Puppy and me to Ashford Stud, where we had an appointment with a celebrity. My grandfather has a friend who owns some shares of a very famous thoroughbred. John drove us through the gated farm entrance, and then we waited. You can't rush a celebrity. We stood in the hot June sun. I found some more horse graves to look at. Puppy and John reviewed the highlights of the past few days. A stable hand brought out Giant's Causeway, another legendary horse; we took some photos with him so as not to make him feel bad, but he wasn't the one we were there to see.

And then, finally, there he was: 2015 Triple Crown winner American Pharoah.

I remember where I was when he won. It was June 6, 2015, and I was at my five-year college reunion. One of my best friends from Wellesley, Cary, suggested we take a break from the afternoon cookout to turn on her laptop so we could watch the Belmont Stakes. Cary grew up riding horses in Virginia, and she had closely followed American Pharoah's wins the preceding weeks at the Kentucky Derby and the Preakness. If the horse won this final race, she emphasized, he would be the first winner of the Triple Crown since Affirmed in 1978. We gathered around her laptop in a dorm room, peering at the tiny screen, sipping warm beers. At the opening of the gates, Cary gritted her teeth—American Pharoah didn't have a strong start. The horse and the jockey seemed lost in the pack, and to my untrained eye it looked like it could be anyone's race. But within twenty seconds American Pharoah had pushed his way forward. Cary took in a sharp breath, and I found myself tightly clutching my can, eyes on the video stream. The thoroughbred surged forward, and forward, until, a minute and a half in, he was ahead by three-quarters of a length, then a full length, and then two lengths. I felt like I was watching footage of Secretariat all over again. I remembered the ancient Egyptian belief that animals oc-cupy the space between the human world and the divine, and as the bay stallion soared ahead to the finish line, end-ing the thirty-seven-year Triple Crown drought, I couldn't help but think I was watching a creature not of this earth. Cary screamed as American Pharoah crossed the wire, and I found myself crying. I had never met this horse, I didn't know this horse, but something about watching him run, about seeing that victorious win, the realization that I was witnessing part of history in the middle of a Saturday after-noon on my college campus—I felt overwhelmed by emo-tion. Cary would later describe watching American Phar-oah's Belmont win as "one of the most magical days of the last decade."

All of those feelings hit me again as the groom led American Pharoah out to meet me and Puppy. My grandfather didn't think twice. He got right in there, patting the famous horse's mane. (For the rest of the day he would crow, "I never thought I would touch a Triple Crown winner!") But I didn't follow Puppy's lead. I held back, frozen. I was in awe. Overwhelmed. I would spend the rest of the day kicking myself, thinking, *I can't believe I didn't touch a Triple Crown winner.* But I had been paralyzed. I kept flashing back to that footage of him flying fast at the Belmont, so far ahead of all the other horses. Despite the hot Kentucky summer sun, I was chilled.

"He knows he is a champion," Puppy's friend had said of the Triple Crown winner. He really does. American Pharoah is calm, confident. He's the hot guy at the party who knows he's the most attractive person in the room. He turned his head slowly and looked into my eyes. I stopped, arrested by his athletic beauty. Maybe I was a little bit afraid to touch an animal worth that much money — American Pharoah's stud fee is $200,000. But more than that, I know that I was overcome by the thrill of celebrity. I suddenly got why millions of people came to see Man o' War in his retirement years at Faraway Farms. I already understood the idea of making a pilgrimage to a grave or a memorial to pay respect — people need closure. But I was blown away when I saw American Pharoah. So handsome, so athletic, so alive. His muscles rippled. I could see the air moving through his nostrils, his chest rising and falling. He focused a steady brown-eyed gaze in my direction. Maybe seeing a famous live animal was even better than seeing the grave of a famous dead one. Maybe it was just the contrast of seeing American Pharoah, so very alive, so well, so clearly breathing, after spending two days studying the graves of very dead horses. He was a glowing specimen of health. He was a spark of energy, some Mother Nature magic. The entirety of my notes from our visit to Ashford Stud consists of one sentence: *American Pharoah is so beautiful.* Perhaps I was afraid to touch him because of the overwhelming life that pulsed through him. Or maybe I didn't touch him because I didn't want to get attached—at least, not even more attached. Because I already knew, as Puppy rubbed his hands all over the horse's mane, that one day American Pharoah would die, and I would grieve for him.

Felines & Feelings

ABOUT FIFTEEN YEARS after Chuckie died on my watch, Meri sent a text: "Look what I got at the farmers' market!" I expected a bouquet of fresh sunflowers or a jar of local honey or a particularly beautiful piece of broccoli. Instead she sent a photo of a kitten. The hamster kid was now a cat lady.

"His name is Clark! Because I got him at Clark Park," she explained. Meri was living in Philadelphia at the time for grad school, near a place called, apparently, Clark Park.

"Aw!" I texted back. Little did I know I had just met my new nemesis.

Don't get me wrong: it's not that I don't like cats. I just never learned how to be at ease around them. While my mom is super allergic to dogs, her cat allergies are basically fatal. I never even tried for a kitten. Growing up, some of my aunts had cats, some of my friends had cats, I even get along pretty well with one particular feline named Buster, though he acts a lot like a dog — but it wasn't quite enough for me to understand how they work.

So when Meri got Clark, I didn't have a lot of cat experience. But I had hope. I love animals, right? I've had so many pets, right? How hard could it be to get a cat to love me or for me to love a cat?

But then I met Clark.

Clark is a brown-and-black striped cat, a Bengal variety, sleek and elegant, with the looks of a small jungle tiger, and he acts like one, too. The first time I met him was when I went to visit Meri in Philadelphia for her birthday with our friends Tuck and Liz. Tuck and Liz slept on an air mattress on the floor of Meri's living room, and I curled up in her bowl chair, and, let me tell you, Clark did not like having new people in his house. In particular, he seemed to have a problem with all the extra toes hanging around. No one slept at all that weekend as Clark systematically attacked our feet, over and over, all night long. I felt in my chest something I'd never felt toward a pet. Was this . . . hate?

It was safe to say that everyone was a little afraid of Clark, and Clark didn't seem to like anyone except Meri — but he could even turn on her. Meri once startled him coming into the kitchen for a glass of water and Clark scratched at her face, slashing the skin above her eye. Clark was wild, had attitude, and was quick to bite. But all that changed when Meri's mom got sick.

Dori was diagnosed with ovarian cancer in 2014. Dori, who had so gracefully handled the dead-hamster phone call, who commiserated with my mom over having pets just for the sake of their daughters, who had been like an aunt to me, was sick. Everything about Dori having cancer was awful. Except that Clark was transformed.

Meri moved back in with her parents to help take care of her mom, and she brought Clark with her. The dogs that Dori and Meri's dad, Steve, adopted after Meri's childhood dog Jasper died — Dudley and Albie — were both gentle and kind to Dori throughout her treatment. After dinner, they would sit on her lap for hours at a time. Even Albie, who had behavioral problems, stayed calm when he was with Dori.

"Suddenly he won't leave my side," Dori told my mom about the dog. It would be the last phone call they had before Dori died. "Usually Albie only has eyes for Steve, but he's always next to me now." She paused. "He knows something's wrong."

But dogs are known for things like that. They're loyal, they're kind — think of those Saint Bernards pulling people out of snowdrifts in the Alps. Dogs can even be trained to sniff out cancer cells and the coronavirus. Cats are not known for any of these qualities. And yet Albie and Dudley's sensitivity and compassion were nothing compared with Clark's.

Wild, fierce, unpredictable Clark spent every evening on Dori's side of the bed. When Dori was downstairs, he stayed in the spot, as if keeping it warm for her return. But even more remarkable than that: when Meri and Dori sat together watching television or talking or reading, Clark would snuggle with Dori. Meri had always been the only person he showed any affection for, but suddenly he chose Dori over her. Dori was a little bit hesitant at first — she knew what Clark was like — but eventually she relaxed. Clark kept her warm, calm, and comfortable. The devil cat with a heart of gold.

And here's the part I think about most: when Dori went to the hospital one day in April 2016, Clark immediately stopped his bed-warming routine. Meri and her dad didn't realize this would be the end for Dori — Meri went to work that morning thinking everything was fine — but somehow Clark sensed Dori wasn't coming back. She died in the hospital that night, just over two years after her diagnosis, and Clark knew right away. That first night without Dori, Clark turned his attention back to Meri. He warmed her bed instead; he cuddled with her every night. He seemed to know that it was Meri who needed him now.

Marc Bekoff writes in his book *Strolling with Our Kin*

that "in order to talk about the world of other animals, we have to use whatever language we speak." I understand this to mean that if we want to describe animal behaviors, our only choice is to use the words we have at our disposal, the same words we use to describe human feelings and actions. In Clark's case, I saw him showing kindness, being affectionate, acting protective. Scientists who study animals work hard not to use such anthropomorphic language when talking about other species; they try not to project human feelings and attitudes onto their subjects. I understand this—how can we ever really know what another being is thinking, or how their brain works, or how they understand the world? It seems unfair to burden other species with all of our human baggage.

But at the same time, it's natural to look at a fellow creature and try to figure them out based on what you know and feel yourself. As Leslie Irvine writes in *If You Tame Me,* "all human attempts to understand and describe any phenomena occur from the human point of view." When your dog goes running up to a friend you haven't seen in a long time, you say, "She's so happy to see you!" What you're really saying is "I'm so happy to see you!" It's also just fun to do: "Omg my cat *loves* pizza!" or "My iguana is really moody today!" You can write scripts for them, make up stories, develop whole plotlines. I can't count the number of times I've overheard a person in a park say, "Ooh, someone has a crush!" about two dogs that are playing together. It's weird, but it's joyful. And until our pets can learn to speak our language (or we learn theirs), our own words are the best thing we've got to understand the situation.

To that end, in *How Animals Grieve,* Barbara King shares stories she's gathered as an anthropologist about the grief or, at least, grief-like behaviors of animals. King writes of a cat, Willa, who fell into terrible distress after her cat-sister, Carson, died. Willa and Carson spent the entirety of their lives together, and they slept curled in toward each other, two half moons. King describes Willa's response when Carson became sick and died: "With a glance at the soft, warm cushion, she lets out a wail . . . She looks, and looks; another wail escapes her. It's sudden and terrible, not a noise one would expect from a cat."

Grief between animals can transcend species. In *Mitz: The Marmoset of Bloomsbury,* Sigrid Nunez describes Virginia and Leonard Woolf's pet monkey, Mitz, appearing listless and melancholy after the death of the Woolfs' dog, Pinka. Several animal websites reported a story about a cat named Scout Kitty who became deeply bonded to the family dog, Charlie, when she was a kitten. She could sleep only when cuddled up next to him. They would eat together, play together, nap together. When Charlie died of cancer, Scout seemed lost and sad. Her owner put videos of Charlie on an iPad and set it up in the dog's old bed. Scout now watches the videos of Charlie and then curls up in the bed next to the iPad to sleep.

King also writes of Tarra, an elephant at the Elephant Sanctuary in Tennessee. For eight years her best friend was a little stray dog named Bella. The giant elephant and the tiny dog roamed the sanctuary grounds as a pair, inseparable, and they became sensations because of their extreme size difference. They were even featured in several picture books. Tarra and Bella didn't seem to care — friendship can transcend size, shape, color, and species. But as King points out, with great love comes great grief. Bella was killed one night, seemingly by a pack of coyotes. Tarra found her friend's body and carried it back to the barn. After the staff of the Elephant Sanctuary buried Bella, they regularly found evidence that Tarra would visit her grave — fresh elephant dung, DNA-matched to Tarra, and an elephant footprint directly over the small dog's final resting place. Elephants are known to visit and spend time with one another's corpses, laying branches and leaves and soil on the dead elephant's body — Tarra was treating Bella as she would a tiny elephant.

These are all examples of animals that seemed to act as equals — siblings, friends, colleagues. There are cases of animals grieving their offspring; an orca known as Tahlequah or J35 mourned her calf, pushing along her baby's body with the rest of the pod for seventeen days. And sometimes,

it seems, an animal can have a pet of its own. Koko the gorilla was born in 1971 and died in 2018, as I was writing this
book. On her birthday in July 1984, Koko was allowed to
choose a kitten from a litter as her present. She picked out
a gray-and-white little guy, whom she named All Ball because apparently the gorilla thought the kitten looked like
a little ball, and she liked to rhyme words in sign language.
Koko and All Ball were inseparable — somehow the kitten
was not afraid of the 230-pound gorilla, and the two would
chase each other around Koko's enclosure for at least an
hour every day. But one day, All Ball escaped from the research facility and ended up on a nearby highway, where
she was struck and killed by a car. When the researchers explained to Koko what had happened, the gorilla expressed
what seemed like denial about the loss of her pet. "She
acted like she didn't hear us for about ten minutes," said
biologist Ron Cohn. "Then she started whimpering — a
distinct hooting sound that gorillas make when they are
sad. We all started crying together." Koko clearly understood that her kitten friend was not coming back to her,
though it is unclear whether she understood it as death.
"Sleep cat," Koko gestured once she'd stopped crying. Not
that different from how little kids understand death: *Your
pet is now sleeping, forever.*

And of course, if animals can mourn across species, they
can mourn the loss of humans, too. Humans generally out-

live their pets — we have longer life spans — but pets are at times left behind to do the mourning instead. "Dogs are the best mourners in the world, as everyone knows," writes author Joy Williams. Arguably the most famous canine mourner in ancient literature appears in *The Odyssey*. Odysseus has been off fighting in the ten-year Trojan War and then, on his way back, he gets sidetracked for another ten years, keeping him away from home for a cool two decades. All kinds of shenanigans have been going down in Ithaca while Odysseus has been away — his son, Telemachus, has grown into an angsty young man; his wife, Penelope, has been fighting off aggressive suitors; and, most importantly, Odysseus's loyal dog Argos has been hanging on, waiting for his owner to return. When Odysseus finally makes it back to Ithaca, he returns to the city in disguise (long story), and the only one to recognize him is Argos. The dog has been lying on piles of mule and cattle dung for decades, and when he finally sees Odysseus, he is too weak and old to stand, but he drops his ears and wags his tail.* But here's the kicker: Odysseus notices Argos, flicks away a single tear, and then keeps on going, because he doesn't want to give away his disguise. And with that Argos dies. Either Argos was so happy to see his person again that

---

* I mean, of course Argos is too weak and old to stand; in dog years he is, at minimum, 140.

he died from joy, or he was so devastated that Odysseus couldn't say hey after two decades that he died from heartbreak. Or he was just really old. But in any case, he held that vigil for Odysseus, mourning his owner's absence, for twenty whole years. While some may argue with the use of the words "devastated" and "mourning" here, or even "happy" or "joy" or "loyal"—we can't fully understand what is going on in another species's brain—what is indisputable is that pets get left behind by people all the time, and they clearly react to it. In my opinion, it doesn't really matter if an animal is actually grieving or showing affection or bringing comfort or if they are not—if a human perceives that to be the case, and it feels real to them, then it can have real consequences.

Take Oscar, a therapy cat at the Steere House Nursing and Rehabilitation Center, in Rhode Island, who has accurately predicted the deaths of more than a hundred people. Dr. David Dosa, author of *Making Rounds with Oscar* and a doctor at Steere House, has suggested that Oscar is attracted to dying patients because they release some sort of pheromone. Oscar picks up on this chemical change and shows up at the room of the dying person before the staff at Steere House has any idea that the person is so close to the end. But it doesn't really matter why Oscar shows up at a dying patient's room—what matters is that he's there. "I'd like to think Oscar embodies empathy and companionship," writes Dosa. "He is a critical cog in a well-oiled and dedicated health care team." The Steere House staffers do everything they can to make their dying patients as comfortable as possible toward the end, and Oscar's presence helps the staff do that. When Oscar starts to spend time with a patient, the staff can guess what's going to happen next. The physicians, nurses, and aides are able to notify the patient's family that things are looking grim, so they know it's time to come say goodbye. Oscar also provides comfort for older, sick patients who otherwise may have died alone. Families of patients have expressed to Dosa how comforted they felt knowing Oscar was with their loved ones in their last moments. It's the same thing as with Clark—it doesn't really matter if he was consciously choosing to warm Dori's spot on the bed or not. His actions, whatever the motivation, brought both Dori and Meri comfort in those hard final days.

I think what it really comes down to, why we latch on so tightly to these stories, is that we hope this will happen for us when it comes our time to die—that an animal might sense our time of need and bring us comfort and peace, that we'll be loved and missed so much that a pet holds a vigil after our death. It makes the act of dying feel a little less lonely. I believe this is why so many dying people dream of loved ones who have gone before them— regardless of whether they are actual spirits visiting or our subconscious conjuring tricks, it's comforting to feel you will be welcomed on the other side by those you love. Interestingly, terminally ill children often see their dead pets as the welcoming envoys. Dr. Christopher Kerr, a hospice physician, said in an interview in *Authority Magazine* that "although children may not have known an adult who died, most have known and loved animals that have passed . . . Dying children are visited in their dreams by deceased pets that they have loved and lost. In the end the message was the same whether those who returned were animals or humans and all the children said the same thing — that they were going to be ok, that they were not alone and that they were loved." We all just want to know we are loved — both in our lives and in our deaths. Knowing that someone, anyone, will grieve for you after you are gone makes you feel like you are living life right.

Look at Hachiko. Hachiko, an Akita, belonged to Hidesaburo Ueno, a professor at Tokyo's Imperial University. Every day, faithful Hachiko would accompany Professor Ueno to the train station in Shibuya to see him off to work, and every evening faithful Hachiko would return to the train station to greet him on his commute home. But one day in 1925, Ueno unexpectedly died of a cerebral hemorrhage while giving a lecture. Hachiko was waiting for the professor at the station that evening as usual, but he never arrived. Hachiko returned to the train station every evening, waiting for Ueno. Commuters began to notice the dog, bringing him food and water as he kept his watch, which he did until his own death—almost exactly ten years later. By then his loyalty and faithfulness were well known throughout Tokyo, and the city grieved. A wake was held for him in the staff room on the second floor of Shibuya Station, and a statue was erected in his honor outside the station, surrounded by a black-and-white funeral curtain, flowers, and other offerings. Since Hachiko's death in 1935, his statue has become a popular tourist destination and meeting spot; there's even a festival held in his memory every spring. "Hachiko ultimately is not remembered as a family pet but as a national and local symbol," writes Barbara Ambros in *Bones of Contention.*

There are so many animals like Hachiko. A Skye terrier named Greyfriars Bobby spent fourteen years at the grave of his dead owner, John Gray, a night watchman for the Edinburgh City Police. Gray passed away in 1858, and it is believed that Bobby observed the funeral and followed Gray's body. He sat down at Gray's grave and never left (I assume people also brought him food) until Bobby himself died in 1872. He was buried next to his person in the churchyard. Locals were moved by Bobby's loyalty, and the dog's collar and bowl were displayed at the Museum of Edinburgh. Like Hachiko, Bobby got his own statue, erected on a granite pedestal in the Greyfriars churchyard in 1873.

These stories are deeply moving—so much so that some people change their end-of-life plans accordingly. I interviewed Larry Eldridge about the death of his Yorkie, Sparky, over lunch in September 2016. Larry loved his Yorkie deeply—when he sat down at the table, he removed his glasses from a case printed with Yorkshire terriers. As we ate our soup, Larry told me about the shiva-inspired memorial service he'd planned in Sparky's honor when the dog died in 2007. He'd written a poem in Sparky's memory and designed a gorgeous headstone engraved with a photorealistic portrait of Sparky, which sits at the dog's grave at the Pine Ridge Pet Cemetery, in Dedham. Later, he and his wife, Joyce, got a new Yorkie named Tater.

When it became clear that Larry's own death was approaching, he made one final request—to have Tater view his body at the funeral home so the dog would know that Larry hadn't abandoned him. When Larry died, Joyce honored the request and made sure Tater saw his body. I asked Joyce if Larry had known about Hachiko and Greyfriars Bobby. "Oh, yes," Joyce said. "Those stories haunted him."

As this book nears printing, we're over two years into the COVID-19 pandemic, and more than 800,000 Americans have been lost to the virus. A horrific tragedy in itself, especially for the family left behind, which includes pets. All year, rescue organizations have gotten phone calls about neighbors who went to the hospital and never made it out, leaving behind cats, dogs, guinea pigs. There are organizations focused on helping the critically ill care for their pets during times of treatment or hospice, such as Pet Peace of Mind, and there are plenty of amazing shelters that work to re-home animals. At the height of infection in New York City, a pet-specific municipal hotline was created for people to call if they were struggling to feed or pay for their pets' care because of the economic recession brought on by the pandemic, or if they wanted to report that a neighbor's pet was in need of help. New Yorkers could also use the hotline to surrender pets if necessary: in just the first three months of the pandemic, the hotline received 145 requests to surrender pets.

One particularly high-profile case in the greater Boston area was the story of Ms. Jennifer, a fifty-three-year-old tortoise, who was surrendered to the Massachusetts Society for the Prevention of Cruelty to Animals (MSPCA) in May 2020 because her person had died of COVID-19. After an article in the *Boston Globe* publicized the tortoise's case — the novelty of her age distinguished her from other pets surrendered by COVID-19 patients — the MSPCA received more than three thousand inquiries about adopting Ms. Jennifer. But she was just one tortoise. If 67 percent of American households own "some sort of pet," as the American Pet Products Association says they do, and even if the majority of those pets live in households with other family members who would continue care for them if their primary owner died—let's assume that's the case 90 percent of the time—we're still talking about close to 8.2 million households with at least one pet in need of a new home.

One story in particular stays with me. Rana Zoe Mungin, a classmate of mine from Wellesley College and a supremely talented writer, died of complications from COVID-19 on April 27, 2020. Zoe and I had lived in the same dorm when I was a sophomore and she was a first-year—the same dorm where I euthanized and then buried Wanda the fish. Sophomore year, Lee and I were roommates again (she didn't hold Wanda's death against me), and Zoe would come hang out in our room as she and Lee studied for Japanese 101 tests together. After college, Zoe and I had mostly kept in touch through a Facebook group for pet-obsessed alums called Wellesley Wags and Whiskers. Zoe was one of the moderators of the group, always posting about her "twins"—her two pit bulls, Rosie and Bandit. Her photos and stories about the dogs and, later, her cat Luna brought the Facebook group constant joy.

When Zoe became sick with COVID-19, hundreds and hundreds of Wags and Whiskers members posted asking for updates on her health, wanting to know ways they could help, offering to send food and money and even dog toys and cat treats. Watching the comments roll in, I thought about how full of life Zoe's posts were. Having an animal in your home is always about living in the moment and finding delight in the absurd, but Zoe's approach to living with pets especially seemed to embody this.

When Zoe died, I was overcome by the shock of losing one of my peers to COVID, anger that Zoe's health concerns were not taken seriously the first few times she went to the ER, and despair at the loss of this smart, funny, incredible young woman, on behalf of her family, her friends, the Wellesley community, and the literary world. And my heart broke for her pets.

Offers immediately came rolling in to the Wags and Whiskers group to adopt Rosie, Bandit, and Luna if they were in need of a home, and Zoe's friends quickly said the animals were being taken care of by Zoe's family. But as I flipped through Zoe's old photos in the group — a close-up of Bandit's brown-and-white nose — I felt such a loss. I could not comprehend what Zoe's mother and sister, her nephew and nieces, her best friends were feeling, and on top of that, these two sweet pit bulls and this little black cat no longer had their person. I wondered if they knew. I wondered if they were waiting for Zoe to come back.

I felt glad, at least, that the animals were with Zoe's family. She had lived in a multigenerational household in East New York, and her stories about her animals always involved her mother, her sister, her nephew, her nieces. Zoe's pets were part of the family. I imagined that it was a little bit of consistency in an otherwise upside-down, sad, impossibly hard, confusing time for all of them. There are so many things that we hang on to after a loved one — human or nonhuman — dies, to look at and remember them: articles of clothing, clippings of fur, old journals, worn collars, albums of photographs. But when we miss a human, inheriting their beloved pets can carry that person — and our love for them — forward.

Canines & Community

*Y*OU KNOW about the fish. You've heard about the birds and the rodents, the turtles and the horses, the cats that were not mine. It's time to tell you about the dogs. I've been putting them off because of all the pets I've had so far in my life, I've spent the most years with my dogs. I grew up with two, both blond cairn terriers, named Gus and Gwen. Between the two of them, their lives spanned sixteen years. I knew them the longest. I knew them the best. And because of that, their deaths were the hardest of them all.

I got Gus in 1997, the fall after Kiki died, when I started at that new school. I still remember the day I was told we were finally getting a dog: October 13, 1997. I'd been with my grandparents, Nunni and Puppy, at the Topsfield Fair. We ate caramel apples and watched Clydesdale horses with ribbons in their manes trot around a big tent. We studied prizewinning pumpkins and enormous rabbits and luscious orchids. Nunni and Puppy indulged me, as they always did, and bought me anything I asked for—until we came to a display of key chains of dog breeds: I ♡ MY [POODLE, GOLDEN RETRIEVER, YORKIE, ETC.].

"Look!" I said, pointing to one particular key chain, "it's a cairn terrier!"

Cairn terriers had been part of my latest begging-for-a-dog strategy. I'd heard about hypoallergenic dogs from my dad's first wife—Sally, my siblings' mom—who had a cairn terrier named Waldo. After meeting Waldo, I promptly looked up other hypoallergenic dogs—the bichon frise, the poodle, the West Highland white terrier, the Portuguese water dog—and made a list, which I left casually out on the kitchen table. I was open to any and all of them, but I found myself hoping for a cairn terrier. I loved Waldo's jaunty ears, his stubborn streak, his intelligence, and his attitude. The breed also had a gleam of celebrity—Toto in *The Wizard of Oz* was a cairn—and once I learned that the Scottish word *cairn* was pronounced "karen," like my mother's name, it seemed like the best possible breed to win her over.

"Can I get this key chain?" I asked my grandparents.

They exchanged a look, which I interpreted as *We've already bought her so much dumb junk today, why does she need this too?* I put on my most pathetic I'm-your-favorite-granddaughter face.

"Well," said Nunni slowly, choosing her words, "maybe you should wait and get a key chain like that once you actually have a dog. You know? You don't want to jinx it."

I looked at the key chain and sighed. I saw her point.

But still, later that evening, when my parents came to pick me up at my grandparents' house, the first thing I told them about the fair was that I'd seen an I ♡ MY CAIRN TERRIER key chain.

My parents exchanged a look.

My grandparents exchanged a look.

I looked at all these adults and wondered what was going on.

"Well," said my mom. "We have some news, actually. We went to Meredith, New Hampshire, today." I looked at my parents blankly. "We were at a dog breeder. There's a woman in Meredith who breeds cairn terriers. You know, dogs like Waldo."

I remember nothing else after that. I blacked out from joy. My parents had gone to check out the breeder's newest litter, to see how my mom's allergies were around the puppies. Apparently my mom had held one of the cairn pups and she hadn't sneezed once. They hadn't wanted to tell me ahead of time, in case my mom had a bad reaction and they came back empty-handed. Instead, they returned having placed a down payment on that very puppy my mom had held. We were going to pick him up in a month, once he was old enough to leave his parents.

The next month was the longest of my life. I did not sleep at all the night before we were to drive back up to Meredith. By the time we got to the breeder's house, I was completely overwhelmed with excitement. I took a deep breath and went inside and met the puppy that would become our dog Gus. I looked down at his little face, still coated in extra-soft baby fur, and he looked up at me, and I thought: *Everything is going to be different now.* We drove back to Lexington from Meredith, and I held him the entire time. He slept the whole ride back, snuggled into my fleece pullover.

It became clear pretty quickly, though, that Gus only had eyes for Dad. Sure, Dad was the one who walked him the most, who always kept treats in his pockets, who put in the hours training him, but come on—I was the reason he was in our lives in the first place. Didn't Gus owe me one? Our new puppy was also fiercely independent—a trait all terriers are known for, but Gus especially. He loved to run away, make friends with the neighbors, and steal and destroy important items. The dog had a mind of his own, and being my number one soul-mate companion best friend didn't seem high on his list of priorities. But it was fine. I'd worn down my parents for one dog, so getting a second would be easy.

Gwen came on the scene two years later, the summer before I entered sixth grade. I'd started trolling the *Boston Globe* classifieds again, and found an ad for a kennel called Puppies Galore that sold cairn terriers. I convinced my parents to drive to Puppies Galore, "just to look." And there, in the middle of a pile of puppies, was one little female cairn terrier, licking the ear of the dachshund puppy next to her. Dad and I were sold immediately; Mom was not convinced. She said she needed time to think about it. Dad and I sighed; we all got in the car. Mom drove a thousand feet down the road, stopped, turned around, and said, "Oh, fine, go get her." Gwen snuggled up next to me for the ride home, just as Gus had, and then proceeded to puke all over the car door, foreshadowing fourteen years of motion sickness.

But I didn't care. I loved Gwen and all her vomit. I loved Gus, even if maybe he loved Dad or being by himself more. These two dogs were my most loyal friends, constant companions for years.

But nothing in life is constant. Especially not a pet.

This is how Gus died:

In the fall of 2006, when I was eighteen and a first-year

at Wellesley, my parents called to tell me they were going to have to put Gus down. He had frequently had health issues, and lately he'd been having trouble moving his bowels. I hadn't been concerned—Gus always seemed to bounce back. But this time he didn't. My parents tried a surgery to fix the problem—his intestines were no longer contracting properly—but it only seemed to make things worse. He was bleeding when he went to the bathroom, and he'd even stopped eating—his absolute favorite activity. It was the end.

I remember where I was: walking from the academic quad back to my dorm, by the campus art museum. When they told me why they were calling, I sat down hard on the curb. Hot tears washed down my face; I felt the same intense emotion that I'd felt in my grandparents' kitchen the day my parents told me we were getting a dog—except this time it was the opposite.

Mom and Dad picked me up the next day. I spent the afternoon and evening at home, lying on the kitchen floor next to Gus while he slept. I kept asking myself, *What gives us the right to decide this?* I thought about finding those first dead fish, how Mom had explained that they died because "it was their time." But how did we know it was Gus's time? I stayed on the kitchen floor next to Gus until it was very late. *This is his last night on earth,* I kept thinking. *This is our last night with Gus.* I cried myself to sleep.

Gus died on November 7, 2006, a week shy of nine years from the day we got him. Despite being so sick, Gus was still excited to get in the car when we drove him to the vet. Next to eating, going for a ride was his favorite pastime. He wagged his tail and tried to jump into the back seat. *If only he knew where we were taking him,* I thought, already crying. Gus looked out the window for the whole drive. I rubbed his back and looked out with him. When we got to the vet, he jumped out of the car and ran into the animal hospital — despite so many painful surgeries, he still loved everyone who worked there. I couldn't see, my tears were so warm and thick, and then there we were: Gus on a stainless-steel table, the three of us standing around him.

My parents and I each placed our hands on his back, rubbing the wiry hair. My dad clutched a blond fistful of fur tightly. The vet inserted the syringe, and even before it was empty, Gus's knees buckled and he sank. His pink tongue hung out of his mouth, too loose. My vision blurred and the three of us continued to stroke Gus's back as he lay there, his face smooshed into the towels around him, crumpled in an unnatural sleeping position. The warmth was already beginning to leave him, the steady rhythm of his breath was gone. I unclicked the worn blue nylon collar and folded it tightly into my palm. Mom had already left the room and gone out to the car — always one to tamp down her emotions and get back to business. Dad, meanwhile, was sobbing in a way that I hadn't seen since his father died. My dad had had dogs before. He'd seen his dogs die; he'd already had to make difficult calls about euthanasia. I looked at him confused, but he shook his head.

"Every time," he said, "I think it's going to get easier. But every time it's different and awful in its own way."

We had Gus's body cremated—my mom, the one who had never wanted a dog, insisted we pay the extra money to have him cremated individually—and we kept the box of his ashes on the floor next to the fireplace. We weren't sure what to do with them. Six months passed, and then it was Memorial Day weekend: the first days of summer, when my family heads to Fishers Island, when we take my dad's boat off the trailer and put it back into the ocean. Dad checked the weather forecast—calm, sunny, still—and without talking about it, we knew it was time. My parents and I took the ashes out on the boat. The only thing Gus loved to do more than ride in the car was to ride on the boat. He loved to bark at seagulls and striped bass, he basked in all the smells whizzing past his nose, and he gobbled up all those little minnows that big fish would regurgitate on the deck. Dad drove his boat to the lighthouse, his favorite fishing spot, where he and Gus had spent hours together. Slowly, carefully, one by one, my parents and I each took a handful of Gus's ashes and released them into the ocean. We repeated the process until the plastic box was empty and all three of us were crying. Then my dad leaned over the side of the boat to dip his hand in the waves, to rinse off the last bits of ash on his hand.

"Goodbye, Gus," he said, crying again. And as he leaned over, as if to pet the ashes drifting down below the surface, Dad's sunglasses, which had been propped up on top of his head, slipped off and into the ocean.

"Oh, Rich," my mom said through tears. "Those were expensive!"

My dad was crying too hard to say anything.

Mom dipped her hand in next.

"Goodbye, Gus," she said, reaching over the side of the boat. As her fingertips brushed the water, my mom's sunglasses also fell off and into the waves. "Oh my God, really?"

Dad was still crying, but he started laughing, too. "It's Gus!" he said. "He's playing one last prank on us!" I thought of how Gus had learned how to open the screen door of our house and run off on adventures, how he'd chewed up my brand-new fifth-grade social studies textbook, how he'd find and piss off the one skunk in our neighborhood —how he was always up to something. Of course Gus's ghost would launch two pairs of sunglasses into the ocean.

Mom started laughing, and I did, too. "What a jerk!" she said. "Typical Gus!" I shouted.

And then I reached over the side of the boat to dip my

hand in the water, too. But first I took my sunglasses off my head and put them in my pocket. "You're not getting these, Gus!" I said, laughing and crying at once. I dipped my fingers into the water, wiping my eyes with my other hand. Then I sat back down next to my parents and for a few minutes we listened to the seagulls, watching the waves break against the rocks of the lighthouse, remembering Gus.

And this is how Gwen died:

She began slowing down in the years after I graduated from college. We'd been told by one vet that she had Lyme disease, and we dutifully wrapped up baby aspirin in slices of cheese every day so she could eat the cheese and spit the pill out on the carpet. Mom baked whole chickens just for Gwen. She got extra snacks, extra ear scratches — she even got to lounge on the couch.

In May 2013, when I was in grad school, Gwen turned fourteen. By that point, she slept almost exclusively on the sofa, but she had to be lifted on and off. Sometimes she would snap or bite when one of us tried to pick her up — an uncharacteristic behavior that suggested she might be in pain. Then, one day in the middle of June, she stopped eating. I was living with my parents at the time, spending the summer between grad school semesters at their

house on Fishers. I was nannying for a family and working at the island's small letterpress print shop. I had to go
to work that day, so my parents took Gwen by themselves
in my dad's boat—the same one we used to spread Gus's
ashes, the boat poor Gwen hated as much as Gus had loved
it—over to a vet on the mainland, in Noank, Connecticut. The vet suggested a Lyme disease flare-up and pre-
scribed more aspirin. My parents brought her back to the
island. But by the end of the month, Gwen had stopped
drinking water. She was panting and wheezing hard, even
when lying still. Though we didn't say it out loud, Mom,
Dad, and I all knew this wasn't Lyme disease. Later, after Gwen died, we realized we'd each been separately praying that one morning we'd come downstairs and find that
Gwen simply hadn't woken up. None of us wanted to have
to make the call again.

But, deep down, we knew we'd have to. My parents
made another appointment at the Connecticut vet office
for July 3. Mom and Dad suggested that maybe I should
go with them, just in case. I took the morning off work and
we all got on the boat, Mom holding Gwen tightly.

When we docked in Noank, we cut through some
bushes and a ditch by the side of the road to get to the
vet's office, which was, thankfully, walking distance from
the dock. Once we were there, the vet performed a scan
and confirmed what we'd all guessed: Gwen was full of

tumors, and she was hurting. There were two lemon-sized growths blocking up her large intestines, which was why she couldn't eat, drink, or go to the bathroom. The tumors had even metastasized to her lungs, which explained why she'd been having trouble breathing. The vet asked what we wanted to do.

Mom, Dad, and I looked at each other. We were already there. None of us liked the idea of subjecting such a sick, hurting dog to another boat ride, to prolonged suffering.

Gwen had always hated loud noises, thunderstorms, and especially fireworks. She would spend the week leading up to the Fourth of July hiding in the bathroom. We'd known she must be pretty sick not to have moved from her spot on the couch the past few days, even as neighbors tested out flares and Roman candles. We decided that our last gift to her would be to send her off before she had to suffer through another Independence Day.

And just as my dad had promised, putting down Gwen was awful in its own distinct way.

On the boat ride back to the island, I held Gwen — or the shell of her. Mom had said at the vet's that she didn't feel cremation was right for Gwen; our second dog had always been such a homebody, Mom wanted to bring her back to Fishers Island and bury her by the house. Dad and I agreed. On the boat, I cradled her body close, wrapped in several towels. Even though it served no purpose, I tried to protect her from the wind. I felt urine and other fluids leaking onto the towel and my shorts, but I only held her tighter. When we finally got home, we buried Gwen's body in the yard, and later planted a hydrangea bush on top.

So that's how Gus and Gwen died. They were both old and sick. For both we had to make the call to euthanize. Both died on stainless-steel tables in veterinary offices. Both times it was just me and my parents present with them as the veterinarian gave the final injection. My memories of their deaths are heavy with the weight of a terrible decision, cold at the thought of the stainless-steel table, and lonely—feeling like no one else could possibly understand just how awful it all feels.

And yet.

When our pets are alive, they help us establish community. When my parents don't have dogs, they know very few of their neighbors; when they do have dogs, they spend hours on walks around town, chatting with people about their pets, their families, their jobs, their lives. As Julie Beck put it in *The Atlantic,* "dogs do not give a hoot about our elaborate, chilly social dances. They'll interact with whomever they like, thanks very much."

A study from 2008 reported that people are more inclined to help a stranger pick up a handful of dropped coins if the coin dropper has a dog with them. I'm hesitant to talk to strangers by themselves, but if I see a person with a particularly adorable puppy on the subway, or someone walking a rabbit on a leash in the park, the barriers come down. Asking questions about the animal—name, age, breed—is an obvious icebreaker, and there's also a comfort in being able to address the animal first instead of the human—"What's your name?" Wrote Beck: "The dog is a safer target; it probably won't reject you." But more than that, I know right away that this person and I have common ground, a shared interest.

People also use pets as a type of litmus test. Paul M. Vanecko has been a dog walker in the greater Boston area for close to a decade, and he knows right away whether or not a relationship is going to last based on how the person reacts to his line of work. Vanecko says that his relationship with animals began when he could walk. His ancestry is Portuguese, Cape Verdean, Jewish, Armenian, and Native American, and he was adopted into an Irish Czech family. "As I got older, I struggled to feel a natural connection to my family," he explained. So he turned to dogs for emotional support instead. It seemed completely obvious, then, when Vanecko left the corporate world to pursue a career "closer to [his] heart," that it would involve dogs. His very first job, at age twelve, encouraged by his father, was a dog-walking business where he charged fifty cents per half-hour walk. And it was his dad's death that finally pushed him to start his adult dog-walking business. "He couldn't get me to do certain things when he was alive," Vanecko said of his dad, "but after he died, he turned out to be more successful." He said that in leaving the corporate world for dog walking he was able to "unlock the door to something that had been locked up for three decades—my true and absolute joy." He's been walking dogs ever since.

"It took me a lifetime to figure out what made me the most happy," he said of his dog-walking career, and he hasn't let anyone change that. He told me that about three years ago, he had just started dating someone, and the guy came over one night while he was dog-sitting a black Lab mix named Murphy. They both took Murphy for a walk, and when Vanecko bent down to pick up Murphy's poop, he detected a note of disgust from the potential boyfriend. "This guy is embarrassed by what I do for a living?" Vanecko recalled, horrified. I could almost hear him roll his eyes over the phone. "I gave him his walking papers."

As he should, because Vanecko doesn't need those kinds of people in his life—he has so many others. The sheer number of names he rattled off during our conversation—Murphy, Jeb, Grace, Maggie, Tyson, Riley, Zishe—were those of dogs he was currently walking, used to walk, dogs that had long since died. But also, Vanecko spoke about the families of those dogs, the people who would hire him, the people he used to work for, people who had moved, people whose dogs had died and no longer needed his services — he had built an entire community.

I spoke to him in August 2020, about six months into the COVID pandemic, and he told me that he had lost a significant number of his clients — with more people working from home, fewer people needed to hire a dog walker, and with so many people losing work, many couldn't afford a dog walker even if they wanted one. He'd lost two-thirds of his customers. But the ones who remained were the ones that got Vanecko through. Some clients said they no longer needed him to come walk their dogs but continued to send him a weekly check. Other clients just wanted to keep up some semblance of normalcy and asked him to continue to come by to walk their dogs to help them feel like things weren't that weird and different. There were clients who moved away, clients who freaked out that Vanecko might be a vector (even though, arguably, he has one of the safest work environments possible — always outside and always more than six feet away from others because of his gaggle of dogs), but the ones who continued their support were anchors. And in life, during a global pandemic or otherwise, you need all the anchors you can get.

Fran Weil gets this better than anyone. She's the co-founder of Perfect Paws Pet Ministry, out of All Saints

Episcopal Church of the North Shore, in Danvers, Massachusetts. Perfect Paws hosts gatherings once a month where people can bring their pets. These monthly worship services remember pets that have died but also celebrate those that are still with us. Perfect Paws began after Weil and her spouse, Gail Arnold, had to euthanize one of their beloved Westies, named Preston. Weil and Arnold were at church one Sunday morning, and the priest at the time, Thea Keith-Lucas, noticed that they didn't seem like their usual perky selves. Keith-Lucas asked what was wrong, and Fran explained that the vet was coming over later that day to euthanize Preston. That day during mass, Keith-Lucas asked the congregation to pray for Weil, Arnold, and Preston. After the service, Weil recalled, "there wasn't a person in the sanctuary who didn't love us up and hug us." She was inspired to start Perfect Paws Pet Ministry then and there, to see if she could create a group to help people feel less alone in their pet death grief, and with Keith-Lucas's help Weil began hosting the monthly services.

In November 2019, Richie and I went together to one of Perfect Paws services. This was a special gathering—their annual service of remembrance and Thanksgiving for all the animals loved and lost in the past year. An All Souls' mass for pets, in a way. Richie and I were hesitant at first, just showing up—we didn't want to intrude on anyone's space to grieve. But then a woman with a black Lab puppy passed us and opened the door, and the warm light of the rectory spilled out into the dark, harsh, cold November. "You coming in?" she asked, holding the door as the puppy pulled ahead. Richie and I rushed up and entered.

I quickly found Weil—she wasn't hard to spot, the clear belle of the ball. Petite, with short white hair and glasses, and brightly colored clothing, I could hear her joyful voice above all the others when we entered the rectory. Weil knows everyone who comes to Perfect Paws personally—all the humans, all the pets, and all the past pets as well. She remembers stories about animals dead and alive, people dead and alive. She keeps tabs on health problems and life changes, she always checks in on how *you* are doing, and the community she's created through the monthly services is truly exceptional. (And she is quick to downplay her efforts, telling you how "each and every person involved has leaned in to support the ministry.")

Perfect Paws takes place in the rectory hall attached to All Saints. ("Because of the shedding," Weil said.) But something about the cozy church hall, the folding chairs, and the informal vibe only added to the comforting feel. Richie and I stood at the back, not wanting to overstep, but people were friendly and kind and helped us navigate the ceremony, offering us programs and available chairs. Some had pets with them, others did not, but there were well over a dozen animals present, including the black Lab puppy we had seen outside, a gang of Yorkies, two majestic Afghan hounds, and a cat in a carrier.

As we waited for the service to begin, I watched the people and their pets. Humans enthusiastically waved at one another when spotted across the room, people crouched down to get eye level with a puppy, animals ran from person to person—sometimes it was unclear who they belonged to, because they were so at home with everyone there. The woman with the black Lab puppy stood at the front of the room, and now, without her coat on, I could see that she was the Reverend Marya DeCarlen, who was to lead the service.

DeCarlen began with a Native American prayer for healing, and the room softened into a quiet hum. It was not the serious, somber silence of a traditional church service, full as it was with the cozy white noise of dog tags jingling, a puppy's yawn, a rustle as the cat readjusted its position. The soft murmuring of a person to their pet. The occasional woof, followed by a soothing shush. Animals don't take anything too seriously, and in their presence, people can't, either. As the service went on, often dogs would bark or howl—along with the music, or whenever there was clapping—and no one got upset or mad; they just chuckled.

Members of the congregation read Bible passages relating to animals and to grief and loss, and DeCarlen reflected on the loss we feel when losing a pet. We spoke names of animals sick or recently deceased and in need of prayer, and Weil played a slideshow of the pets that had died over the past year. Communion was offered, and some participated and others did not—Perfect Paws is open to people of all beliefs—and acoustic guitar accompanied several songs, including one written about the Rainbow Bridge, the concept that our pets wait for us in a sunny, green meadow "this side of heaven" until we die, and then we all cross the bridge together to spend eternity with one another. Because it was a memorial service, we also lit candles to honor the animals we had lost. I held back at first. It had been more than six years since Gwen died; Gus had been gone thirteen. Aristotle, Chuckie, Kiki, all those fish —gone even longer. What right did I have to go up there and light a candle, when DeCarlen was tearing up talking about the death of her dog just this past year?

But looking at all of those people slowly making their way to the front of the room, taking the time to light candles—seeing the animals at their sides, and hearing the whispered names of the animals they'd loved and lost— something hit me. Just because an animal is gone, even if its death is long in the past, that doesn't mean that pet isn't still part of you. It doesn't mean that the experience of having that pet didn't profoundly change you, or make your life better, or help you become a stronger, happier person.

And even if it's been six years, thirteen years, a whole life-time, those animals still deserve to be honored and remembered.

I went to the front of the room and picked up a long match from the glass jar on the table. As I stood waiting my turn, I thought of all the fish, the birds, the rodents, the turtles. I thought of cats and horses I had met, but I focused on the dogs. When I finally reached the table, I lit my long match and touched it to the wicks of three candles—one for Gus, one for Gwen, and one for Richie's childhood dog Cocoa. Gone, but always with us.

The service concluded with a young man singing "The Place Where Lost Things Go." The song is from *Mary Poppins Returns,* and under usual circumstances I may be quick to dismiss it as cheesy, but something about his voice, the candles, the gentle rustling of the many dogs and one cat—I found myself overwhelmed.

I started crying, and I looked over to see Richie was crying, and as I glanced around the room I realized that almost every person there was in tears. *Gone for good you feared. They're all around you still.* Gus, Gwen, Kiki, Wanda—all around me, in that warm rectory hall in Danvers, Massachusetts, one Sunday in November.

After the service, even though everyone seemed emotionally spent, it also seemed everyone felt better. At least I knew that I felt better. I felt safe in this group, this warm, bright room, full of other animal people who understood what grief over a pet is like. I left feeling deeply grateful and admiring of all the hard work Weil and her group do to make these services happen.

Driving home that evening, I thought more about Weil and all the people we had spoken with that night than I did about the animals I had met. This surprised me—I had been a kid who was more comfortable around animals than people. But I thought about how it was through pets that I had found my people. Meri and I bonded over Chuckie, I cemented my group of friends at Wellesley when we buried Wanda, and—I looked over at Richie as I drove my little blue car down 95 South—I had found a life partner who understands pet death better than anyone. When I met Richie, in January 2012, he and his family had just had to euthanize Cocoa the month before. One of the first things we talked about was our dead dogs. From the moment we began talking, I knew that he was a person who understood what it was like to skip class or work to curl up in your bed and cry about your pet dying; he would never laugh if you shed a tear over an animal. I knew right away that Richie was someone who gets it.

So, the year I turned thirty-one, when Richie asked what I wanted to do for my birthday, I knew immediately: rent a cabin in the White Mountains and visit Dog Mountain. Richie, of course, was not surprised, and, of course, he completely understood. I had been talking about wanting to see the place for as long as I had known about it. Dog Mountain, in St. Johnsbury, Vermont, was founded by artist and dog lover Stephen Huneck, famous for his woodblock prints of his black Lab, Sally. People go to Huneck's property to walk their dogs freely, and Dog Mountain hosts large parties each season for humans and canines alike. But Huneck also created a beautiful small chapel, where people leave photos of their deceased dogs, write them notes, pay tribute to the animals they've loved.

I thought I knew what to expect as Richie and I drove on 93 North into the middle of New Hampshire, flying through the White Mountains toward Vermont. I had seen images of the chapel, I got the Dog Mountain email newsletters, I had read Huneck's picture book *The Dog Chapel*. I wiped the lens of my camera and readied my notebook to jot down my observations.

I drove my car up a bright, snowy hill onto the Dog Mountain property. The sky was a sharp blue, and the chapel's white steeple, in the style of a typical New England Georgian church, glowed a crisp white against the December sky. The building was small — maybe five hundred square feet. *That's it?* I couldn't help but think as we got out of the car. I wiped my camera lens again as Richie and I walked up the hill toward the chapel. WELCOME, the sign outside read. ALL CREEDS ALL BREEDS NO DOGMAS. Four carved wooden dogs stood by the entrance, and festive red ribbons were pinned to each of the doors. Richie and I looked at each other — did we just go in? I paused, but reminded myself of how long I had been reading and learning about pet death — not just for this book but over the course of my whole life. I knew what to expect. I got this. I opened the door to the chapel.

And I immediately started crying.

Thousands of notes, thousands of photos. I didn't know where to look first. There were Post-it Notes scrawled on with Sharpie, there were handwritten notecards, there were long typed letters. There were photographs printed from film and photographs printed out on computer paper. Notes written on index cards, Tibetan prayer flags printed with dogs, tennis balls, license tags, bandannas. It was in the thirties in St. Johnsbury that day, and the Dog Chapel does not have heat, but I knew the chills I felt were not from the weather. Sunlight streamed through the stained-glass windows, which portrayed a yellow Lab with angel wings and a halo. Four benches carved with retrievers faced the front of the room. I sat down heavily on one of them and wiped my face. I'd been to so many pet cemeteries at this point, spoken to so many pet caretakers and vets about painful animal death moments, had watched videos on YouTube of euthanasia, had even managed to rewatch *All Dogs Go to Heaven* without shedding a tear. And yet, every time, this was what bowled me over: so many people love their pets, so much.

I sat on the bench and flipped through one of the books displaying even more notes and photos—the walls were overflowing. Richie and I had been alone in the chapel when we first entered, but another couple came in with two spaniels. One dog wandered up to me and I scratched his ears. On Dog Mountain, it is not only not weird to become friendly with strangers' dogs, but actively encouraged. "You're a good boy," I said as the brown-and-white dog buried his nose in the side of my leg. "What's your name?" I asked him as I flipped his dog tag over to look.

Gus.

My eyes filled up and I swallowed hard. Of all the names. I looked up at the stained-glass window with the dog angel. I took a deep breath.

I miss you, too, Gus, I thought. *Thanks for saying hi.*

I stayed in the chapel a while longer, after Richie needed to go outside to collect himself, after the couple and their dogs left, and I thought about how many people had made the journey to this one specific place to reflect on and memorialize and remember their pet. I wished that anyone who had ever felt alone in their grief over their animal, anyone who felt like a weirdo for feeling such excruciating hurt at the death of their pet, who wasn't sure if they were a freak, could see these walls with the thousands and thousands of photographs and notes. There are so many people who love their animals. There are so many people who have felt a connection to their pets that was as profound, maybe even more profound, than their connections to other people. But the irony is that, in order to move through your grief over your pets, you need, more than anything else, other humans. Other people who get it. Other people who will hold your hand and cry over a dog that died thirteen years ago, people who will reassure you that every time is different and awful in its own way. A sad ending doesn't mean the whole experience isn't worth it, and you need other people to help remind you of that.

I took a scrap of red paper and a black Sharpie and wrote out the names: Gus, Gwen, and Cocoa. *Thanks for everything,* I added at the bottom. *Love, E.B. & Richie.*

Remember: the photos, the notes — they are many layers thick.

Epilogue

ALMOST TWO DECADES after I learned about the pet cemetery next to my high school, I found myself back there—this time holding the leash of a very much alive dog.

Richie had told me on our first date, in the winter of 2012, that he could never have another dog again, that Cocoa's death the month before had been too hard. I filed this away as a potential deal-breaker but kept seeing him. For the first couple of years, he remained resolute. I didn't think much of it, because at the time I was living in New York and couldn't have a pet in my apartment anyway. It also wasn't as if Richie *hated* animals—his kitchen had a large aquarium, full of plants and gouramis, that he carefully and gently tended to. I watched how he took care of his fish. I guessed that he was just taking his time to nurse the rawness of his grief over Cocoa.

Then, somewhere around 2014, he began to say maybe he would be okay with *me* getting a dog, a dog that he just *happened* to live with—but he wouldn't love it, definitely not, no way. I said okay and didn't press it. By this point I had moved from New York back up to the Boston area, and I was living in an apartment in Cambridge where I technically wasn't supposed to have pets, but I had a secret pet tortoise. I had found him on Craigslist. A posting by a woman in central Massachusetts, saying that he had been her daughter's pet when the girl was younger, but now she was a teenager who had lost interest in the terrapin. Richie, of course, came with me, and we drove the hour to meet the woman and her boyfriend. Her apartment was crowded with children and cats, but there, on a coffee table in the middle of the living room, right under the television, was the little guy in his tank. The woman picked him up. Unlike Aristotle, who had been wild and neurotic, this tortoise stuck his head farther out of his shell and looked around. He stretched his brown forearms, dotted with the characteristic red-orange scales of a red-foot. She handed him to me, and I couldn't help but flash a shit-eating grin as I rubbed the top of his smooth head.

"He's very curious and friendly," she said. "No one is paying enough attention to him here. I just want him to have a good home, you know?" I nodded. The woman kept talking—about the tortoise's age, his love of arugula, his hatred of kale, how her daughter was mostly living at her dad's house now anyway. Richie listened, but I was star-struck.

"Does he have a name?" I asked.

"Terrence," she said.

I loved it.

Back in Cambridge, Terrence took up residence in a large wooden enclosure—a "turtle table" that Richie and I built ourselves—next to the desk in my apartment. He quickly established himself as a member of the household, roaming the floor of the condo when I let him out of his tank. Terrence would walk laps from the bedroom to the kitchen and back, and when the weather was warm, he enjoyed pacing back and forth on the balcony. When Terrence got tired of walking, he would find a quiet place to fall asleep: under the bed, behind the toilet, next to Richie's bass.

And then, a little while after that, after Richie moved in with me and Terrence, after he had set up his fish tank in the Cambridge apartment, Richie started saying that, well, it was probably inevitable that he'd become friendly with my hypothetical future dog at least. I smiled to myself and tried not to feel too smug.

At this point it had been about five years since Gwen died and, at the beginning of summer 2018, my mom casually mentioned that she had been poking around on Petfinder. I felt a sharp burst in my chest. I was thirty years old, but suddenly I felt twelve, nine, seven again. It was the same feeling I'd had when I first held that cardboard box containing Kiki, or when I cradled baby Gus at the breeder's house in New Hampshire. My heart picked up speed, my eyes began to glow, but I took a deep breath and tried to play it cool.

"Oh?" I said.

"It's just for fun," my mom jumped to say. "I mean, there's too much going on right now. We definitely couldn't get a dog."

I nodded, trying to keep my breathing even.

"It would have to be the perfectly right dog, anyway," she said. "You know how I'm allergic to everything. I'd need a purebred, and when do purebreds ever show up at a rescue?"

I nodded and said, "Well, just keep looking, right? Maybe something will turn up." I exhaled hard.

Two months later, my parents texted me a photo of the two of them holding a five-year-old, red-gold cairn terrier named Honey. A purebred, Honey had been rescued from a backyard breeder who bred her nonstop for three years and then dumped her at a shelter. I zoomed in on the scruffy little dog, and then I zoomed into each of my parents' faces. Both my mom and dad were flashing full smiles, spread wide across their faces, and was that . . . was my mom crying? I smiled to myself. I did it—I had turned Mom into a full-on dog lady. Richie and I met Honey a few days later, and as I watched him scoop up the little terrier and snuggle her into his arms, I guessed Richie was ready again. I thought of one of my favorite pieces of dead-pet literature, *The Last Will and Testament of an Extremely Distinguished Dog,* by Eugene O'Neill, written from the point of view of O'Neill's deceased Dalmatian Blemie. In the short text, Blemie speaks to his owners from beyond the grave and tells them to get another dog: "Now I would ask her, for love of me, to have another. It would be a poor tribute to my memory never to have a dog again." I believe that Gus and Gwen would both want the same. Opening our hearts to Honey doesn't diminish the memory, or the love we felt, for our previous pets. That summer at Fishers Island, standing at Gwen's grave, as Honey sniffed around, I felt Gwen approved of this new family member. As Blemie says: "No matter how deep my sleep I shall hear you, and not all the power of death can keep my spirit from wagging a grateful tail."

Two years later, in summer 2020, the pandemic was fully raging. Unsure of how long it would continue and wanting more outdoor space and the ability to have pets legally, Richie and I decided to buy a house. And the first thing we wanted to do after we moved? Adopt a dog. "Hey, cutie!" Richie would shout as we scrolled through photos of adoptable dogs. "What's your story? Want to come live with us?"

Which is how we ended up back at the pet cemetery. In high school, I had always paid more attention to the graves of all the dead pets—I kind of forgot that the cemetery was owned and operated by the Animal Rescue League of Boston, whose whole deal is trying to help alive pets find homes. One Friday in October 2020, I was doing my usual cycle through all the adoption websites—the shelters were low on available dogs, thanks to the COVID puppy boom—and I happened to see that the Animal Rescue League had just posted four mutts that had been shipped up from a rescue in Florida. I was especially intrigued by a gray terrier mix with big triangular ears, like the bat in the animated movie *Anastasia.* I called the shelter for more information.

"Oh," the shelter staff member said when she answered, "those dogs are already on hold for adoption." I sighed, disappointed. A typical pandemic pet story—impossible to adopt in a climate where everyone is working from home and depressed, just looking for a new furry friend to make their lives a little less bleak. "Wait, sorry," the staff member went on, "only three are on hold. One of them is still available."

"Who's left?" I asked, my heart rising a little bit.

"There's a gray guy, with big bat ears."

My heart soared. I answered the staffer's application questions, explained about my experience with dogs, and within thirty minutes Richie and I were scheduled to meet this gray bat dog the coming weekend.

"Do you know where the shelter is?" the staffer asked at the end of our call. "The dog is at our Dedham location. The one with the pet cemetery." Oh, I knew.

And then there we were. Richie and I said we were just going to look—that maybe this dog wouldn't be the right fit for us, or he might make Richie sneeze, or maybe the dog wouldn't like us—but we both knew we were kidding ourselves. As soon as that gray bat dog walked into the meet-and-greet room, as soon as he got over his initial nervousness and then came right over and licked Richie's face and then mine, we knew we were done.

"Hey, buddy," Richie kept repeating, rubbing the dog's back as the little gray guy leaned into his shins. I sat on the floor, overwhelmed. It had been such a sad, hard year, full of so much grief and loss, but here, seeing this little gray dog pick up a toy and squeak it joyfully, tossing it into the air, watching him run back and forth between me and Richie, I felt my heart cracking open. The Animal Rescue League staff member asked if we wanted to take the dog for a walk, and Richie and I said yes.

We exited the building and followed the path to the oldest part of the cemetery. The fall sunlight filtered through the trees, canopying over the mossy sculptures of nineteenth-century dogs and the lichen covering the names Fluffy and Scrappy. The dog sniffed the old headstones, his one white paw gently poking at the dirt. Richie and I stopped for a moment to sit on a stone bench in a little mausoleum; the dog sat on the stone floor and looked up at us. His brown-yellow eyes studied my face and then Richie's as we looked back at him. His big ears folded against his head and then swiveled around to listen to the squirrels doing parkour on the stones nearby. The dog seemed serious and contemplative, as though he understood what was happening in this moment, how everything was about to change.

"Well?" Richie said, addressing the dog. "Do you want to come home with us and be our friend?"

The answer was obviously yes.

We named him Seymour, after the most loyal cartoon dog on television.* He loves chasing tennis balls and tracking squirrels. He barks whenever anything is moved out of place. He is nervous around large pumpkins and sewer drains. Seymour makes friends with every mail carrier, delivery person, and construction worker he meets. His tail starts wagging as soon as he hears the ding of Richie's bicycle bell when he gets home from work. He naps on the

---

* Fry's dog in *Futurama*. See the episode "Jurassic Bark."

floor by my feet as I write these words. As he snores away, I am reminded of how essayist Durga Chew-Bose writes of her dog, Willis: "I want to trace every surface where he's rested his chin, because one day he'll be gone, and I'll want to look around and see chin prints. Chins remembered. Heartbeats at my feet."

Having a dog is not easy, of course. It's not without frustration or worry. After waking up every hour all night long to take Seymour out during ten days that he had terrible diarrhea, I began to wonder why I had brought this on myself. When Seymour was diagnosed as heartworm-positive, which involved a highly stressful five-month treatment process, I asked what I had gotten myself into. When Seymour barks and lunges after the garbage truck, I have a violent vision of him being crushed under the wheels and feel my heart seize. In the first week we had him, Richie and I tried to trim Seymour's nails ourselves, and when we cut too close to the quick and the dog started bleeding, I felt myself grow faint. I kept waking up that night to check on Seymour, to make sure he wasn't drowning in a pool of his own blood.

One day when I was walking Seymour in my neighborhood, he saw a squirrel across the street and ran into the road.

"No!" I screamed. Seymour cowered and his big ears flattened against his head, his tail between his legs. "You can't do that! You'll get hit by a car!" My voice was getting louder as Seymour looked up at me, worried. "Stop it! I love you too much!"

The responsibility, the weight, of making sure Seymour is alive and healthy and happy is overwhelming sometimes. And, unlike a human baby, he will never grow up into an adult who can take care of himself and strike out on his own. Richie and I are tied to this dog until the moment of his death. Sometimes when Seymour is sleeping, I pet his back and calculate how old I will be when he inevitably dies — mid- to late forties if I'm lucky. I wonder if it will be easier for me to handle then, to cope with Seymour's death, ten or fifteen years in the future. And then I remember my dad crying as we put down Gus and Gwen, and I already know the answer. It never gets easier. Every time is different and awful in its own way. But maybe it's that weight that is exactly what makes it worth it.

There's a Bhutanese folk expression that says in order to be a happy person, one must contemplate death five times every day. Perhaps we love our pets so much not despite but *because* they remind us of death. They're a daily embodiment of how short life is, how important it is to be present in every moment.

It's hard to think about, but it's part of life. And whenever I get too hung up on the sad future, when I sink too deeply into those heavier parts of existence, it's Seymour who reminds me to enjoy the here and now. One time, as I was working on a particularly difficult part of this book, I started crying. There are just so many ways to let down an animal, so many ways to screw up. The stories of people filled with guilt—the accidents, the misdiagnoses, the mistakes—were always the hardest for me to hear. I was sitting at my desk, staring at Microsoft Word, feeling awful, when suddenly I heard squeaking. The noise got louder and louder, and then Seymour burst into my office, shaking his favorite stuffed toy fox. In two quick spins, he flung the toy up onto my desk and it landed squarely on my keyboard, bringing me back to the present moment. All I could do was laugh. There are a lot of things to worry about when it comes to having a pet—it's so easy to let your anxiety rob you of moments of joy. But as Seymour spun around, waiting for me to throw the fox back to him, so thrilled just to be in my presence, playing together, I thought that maybe, just maybe, I'm doing okay. I'm doing the best I can, and Seymour, at least, thinks that is pretty great. I'm already the person Seymour thinks I am.

When my Wellesley classmate Zoe, who died of complications from COVID in April 2020, was interviewed in 2018 in our alum magazine about her pit bulls Rosie and Bandit, she was asked what she thought the value was in having dogs in your life. Zoe explained that they "add depth in a world that I think needs it, and, I think, a flash of reality. You know, the seasons are changing. The dogs need to go out. Time is passing. We're still here, still going strong. We're going to make it."

I pet Seymour's big gray ears and he looks up at me, staring with that same intense gaze as always. *We're here,* he says. *We're strong. We're going to make it.*

Selected Sources

Below is just a selection of the many excellent sources I referred to as I was writing this book. Please check them out for even more information about pet death and grief.

If you are having a particularly hard time coping with the death of your pet, please do not hesitate to reach out to the Tufts Pet Loss Support Hotline at 508-839-7966. I hope that if you take away one thing from this book, it is that you are not alone.

INTRODUCTION

American Pet Products Association. *2019–2020 APPA National Pet Owners Survey.* Stamford, CT: American Pet Products Association, 2019.

Baker, Steve. *Picturing the Beast: Animals, Identity, and Representation.* Manchester, UK: Manchester University Press, 1993.

Banks, T. J. "Why Some People Want to Be Buried with Their

Pets." *Petful,* August 28, 2017. Accessed March 18, 2019. https://www.petful.com/animal-welfare/can-pet-buried/.

Berger, John. *Why Look at Animals?* London: Penguin Books, 2009.

Borrelli, Christopher. "Pet Cemeteries Grow More Popular: 'Pets Are Family.'" *Chicago Tribune,* November 1, 2017. Accessed March 19, 2019. https://www.chicagotribune.com/entertain ment/ct-ent-pet-cemeteries-20171026-story.html.

Brulliard, Karin, and Scott Clement. "How Many Americans Have Pets? An Investigation of Fuzzy Statistics." *Washington Post,* January 31, 2019. Accessed November 22, 2019. https://www.washingtonpost.com/science/2019/01/31/how-many -americans-have-pets-an-investigation-into-fuzzy-statistics/.

Cochrane, Emma. "The Mariah Carey Story." *Smash Hits* (UK), June 19, 1996.

Danovich, Tove K. "The Very Cute, Totally Disturbing Tale of the American 'It' Dog." *New York Magazine,* April 12, 2021. Accessed November 6, 2021. https://nymag.com/article /2021/04/the-totally-disturbing-tale-of-the-american-it-dog .htm.

Jacquet, Jennifer. "Human Error." *Lapham's Quarterly,* July 17, 2016. Accessed November 6, 2021. https://www.lapham squarterly.org/disaster/human-error.

Kriger, Malcom D. *The Peaceable Kingdom in Hartsdale: A Celebration of Pets and Their People.* New York: Rosywick Press, 1983.

Martin, Edward C., Jr. *Dr. Johnson's Apple Orchard: The Story of America's First Pet Cemetery.* Paducah, KY: Image Graphics, 1997.

Martin, Edward C., III. *The Peaceable Kingdom in Hartsdale: America's First Pet Cemetery.* Hartsdale, NY: Hartsdale Pet Cemetery, 2013.

Nussbaum, Emily. "Fiona Apple's Art of Radical Sensitivity." *New Yorker,* March 16, 2020. Accessed November 6, 2021. https://www.newyorker.com/magazine/2020/03/23/fiona-apples-art-of-radical-sensitivity.

Simpson, Dave. "Why Fiona Apple Is Right to Cancel Her Tour for Her Dying Dog." *The Guardian,* November 21, 2012. Accessed November 6, 2021. https://www.theguardian.com/music/musicblog/2012/nov/21/fiona-apple-tour-dying-dog.

Wolfelt, Alan D. *When Your Pet Dies: A Guide to Mourning, Remembering, and Healing.* Fort Collins, CO: Companion Press, 2004.

CHAPTER I: FISH & FOSSILS

American Kennel Club. "Basenji Dog Breed Information." Accessed March 15, 2019. https://www.akc.org/dog-breeds/basenji/.

Bleiberg, Edward, Yekaterina Barbash, and Lisa Bruno. *Soulful Creatures: Animal Mummies in Ancient Egypt.* London: Giles, 2013.

Claybourne, Anna. *Mummies Around the World.* London: A&C Black, 2010.

Finkel, Amy, dir. *Furever.* Olympia, WA: Gaia Indie Films, 2013.

Formanek, Ruth. "When Children Ask About Death." *Elementary School Journal* 75, no. 2 (November 1974): 92–97.

Ikram, Salima. *Beloved Beasts: Animal Mummies from Ancient Egypt.* Cairo: Supreme Council of Antiquities, 2004.

———. *Death and Burial in Ancient Egypt.* London: Pearson Education, 2003.

———, ed. *Divine Creatures: Animal Mummies in Ancient Egypt.* Cairo: American University in Cairo Press, 2004.

Keats, Jonathon. "The Animal Mummy Business." *Discover,* November 10, 2017. Accessed April 18, 2018. https://discover magazine.com/2017/dec/the-animal-mummy-business.

King, Barbara J. *Being with Animals: Why We Are Obsessed with the Furry, Scaly, Feathered Creatures Who Populate Our World.* New York: Doubleday, 2010.

Knapton, Sarah. "Fish Tanks Lower Blood Pressure and Heart Rate." *The Telegraph,* July 30, 2015. Accessed March 15, 2019. https://www.telegraph.co.uk/news/science/science-ne ws/11770965/Fish-tanks-lower-blood-pressure-and-heart-rate.html.

Levinson, Boris M. *Pet-Oriented Child Psychotherapy.* Springfield, IL: Charles C. Thomas, 1997.

Lipton, David. *Goodbye, Brecken.* Washington, DC: Magination Press, 2012.

Lobell, Jarrett A., and Eric A. Powell. "More Than Man's Best Friend." *Archaeology* 63, no. 5 (September/October 2010): 26–35.

Mark, Joshua J. "Dogs in Ancient Egypt." World History Encyclopedia (website). Article published March 13, 2017. Accessed March 18, 2019. https://www.ancient.eu/article/1031/dogs-in-ancient-egypt/.

Matthews, Mimi. *The Pug Who Bit Napoleon: Animal Tales of the 18th and 19th Centuries.* Barnsley: Sword & Pen Books, 2017.

Morton, Ella. "Modern Mummification for You and Your Pet."

Atlas Obscura (blog). *Slate,* March 28, 2014. Accessed November 27, 2019. https://www.slate.com/blogs/atlas_obscura/2014/03/28/salt_lake_city_based_group_summum_will_mummify_you_and_your_pet.html.

National Museum of Natural History. "Eternal Life in Ancient Egypt." Accessed November 6, 2021. https://naturalhistory.si.edu/exhibits/eternal-life-ancient-egypt.

Nir, Sarah Maslin. "New York Burial Plots Will Now Allow Four-Legged Companions." *New York Times,* October 6, 2016. Accessed March 22, 2019. https://www.nytimes.com/2016/10/07/nyregion/new-york-burial-plots-will-now-allow-four-legged-companions.html.

Poston, Hannah Louise. "How a Kitten Eased My Partner's Depression." *New York Times,* August 13, 2015. Accessed November 26, 2019. https://www.nytimes.com/2015/08/16/fashion/how-a-kitten-eased-my-partners-depression.html.

Putnam, James. *Eyewitness: Mummy.* London: Dorling Kindersley, 2000.

Rivenburg, Roy. "Return of the Mummy: A Small Company Has Revived the Egyptian Practice of Preserving Bodies for Posterity." *Los Angeles Times,* January 27, 1993. Accessed November 6, 2021. https://www.latimes.com/archives/la-xpm-1993-01-27-vw-1906-story.html.

Summum. "Animal Mummification Costs." Accessed November 27, 2019. https://www.summum.org/pets/animalcosts.shtml.

Tarlach, Gemma. "The Origins of Dogs." *Discover,* November 9, 2016. Accessed April 18, 2018. discovermagazine.com/2016/dec/the-origins-of-dogs.

Vatomsky, Sonya. "The Movement to Bury Pets Alongside People." *The Atlantic,* October 10, 2017. Accessed March 18, 2019. https://www.theatlantic.com/family/archive/2017/10 /whole-family-cemeteries/542493/.

von den Driesch, Angela, Dieter Kessler, Frank Steinmann, Véronique Berteaux, and Joris Peters. "Mummified, Deified and Buried at Hermopolis Magna—The Sacred Birds from Tuna El-Gebel, Middle Egypt." *Ägypten und Levante/Egypt and the Levant* 15 (2005): 203–44.

Watson, Traci. "In Ancient Egypt, Life Wasn't Easy for Elite Pets." *National Geographic,* May 25 2015. Accessed April 18, 2018. https://www.nationalgeographic.com/history/article/150525-a ncient-egypt-zoo-pets-hierakonpolis-baboons-archaeology/.

Wilcox, Charlotte. *Animal Mummies: Preserved Through the Ages.* Mankato, MN: Capstone Press, 2003.

Wilder, Pana. "The Role of the Elementary School Counselor in Counseling About Death." *Elementary School Guidance & Counseling* 15, no. 1 (October 1980): 56–65.

CHAPTER 2: BIRDS & BONDING

Ackerley, J. R. *My Dog Tulip.* New York: Poseidon Press, 1965.

Bekoff, Marc. *Minding Animals: Awareness, Emotions, and Heart.* Oxford: Oxford University Press, 2002.

Bradley, Theresa, and Ritchie King. "The Dog Economy Is Global—but What Is the World's True Canine Capital?" *The Atlantic,* November 13, 2012. Accessed November 22, 2019. https://www.theatlantic.com/business/archive/2012/11/the -dog-economy-is-global-but-what-is-the-worlds-true-canine -capital/265155/.

Fox, Mem. *Tough Boris.* Orlando, FL: Harcourt, 1994.

Gay, Roxane. "Of Lions and Men: Mourning Samuel DuBose and Cecil the Lion." *New York Times,* July 31, 2015. Accessed November 6, 2021. https://www.nytimes.com/2015/08/01/opinion/of-lions-and-men-mourning-samuel-dubose-and-cecil-the-lion.html.

Herzog, Hal. "Why Kids with Pets Are Better Off." *Psychology Today,* July 12, 2017. Accessed November 6, 2021. https://www.psychologytoday.com/us/blog/animals-and-us/201707/why-kids-pets-are-better.

Irvine, Leslie. *If You Tame Me: Understanding Our Connection with Animals.* Philadelphia: Temple University Press, 2004.

———. *My Dog Always Eats First: Homeless People and Their Animals.* Boulder, CO: Lynne Rienner, 2016.

Olmert, Meg Daley. *Made for Each Other.* Philadelphia: De Capo, 2009.

Parker, Peter. *Ackerley: A Life of J. R. Ackerley.* New York: Farrar, Straus and Giroux, 1989.

Rogak, Lisa. *Dogs of Courage: The Heroism and Heart of Working Dogs Around the World.* New York: St. Martin's, 2012.

Taylor, Ross. "Last Moments." Photo series. Ross Taylor: Photography and Motion Production (website). Accessed October 17, 2021. http://www.rosstaylor.net/photo-stories/last-moments/.

Wroblewski, David. *The Story of Edgar Sawtelle.* New York: HarperCollins, 2008.

Zagorsky, Jay L. "Americans Are Expected to Spend Half a Billion Dollars on Pet Halloween Costumes This Year, and It Shows Just How Society Values Consumerism." *Insider,* October 30, 2019. Accessed November 6, 2021. https://www.bus

inessinsider.com/americans-spend-half-billion-dollars-pet
-halloween-costumes-consumerism-2019-10.

CHAPTER 3: RODENTS & RESPONSIBILITY

Fincham-Gray, Suzy. *My Patients and Other Animals.* New York: Spiegel & Grau, 2018.

Greenwood, Arin. "What Veterinarians Wished You Knew Before Euthanizing Your Pet." *Today,* June 27, 2017. Accessed July 30, 2019. https://www.today.com/series/things-i-wish -i-knew/pet-euthanasia-veterinarians-what-know-when-it-s -time-more-t1113053.

"How Much Does a Veterinarian Make?" *U.S. News & World Report.* Accessed October 17, 2021. https://money.usnews.com /careers/best-jobs/veterinarian/salary.

Kachka, Boris. *Becoming a Veterinarian.* New York: Simon & Schuster, 2019.

Kean, Hilda. *The Great Cat and Dog Massacre: The Real Story of World War Two's Unknown Tragedy.* Chicago: University of Chicago Press, 2017.

Leffler, David. "Suicide Rates Among Veterinarians Become a Growing Problem." *Washington Post,* January 23, 2019. Accessed April 29, 2019. https://www.washingtonpost.com/na tional/health-science/suicides-among-veterinarians-has-be come-a-growing-problem/2019/01/18/0f58df7a-f35b-11e8 -80d0-f7e1948d55f4_story.html.

Nett, Randall J., Tracy K. Witte, Stacy M. Holzbauer, Brigid L. Elchos, Enzo R. Campagnolo, Karl J. Musgrave, Kris K. Carter, et al. "Risk Factors for Suicide, Attitudes Toward

Mental Illness, and Practice-Related Stressors Among US Veterinarians." *Journal of the American Veterinary Medical Association* 247, no. 8 (October 15, 2015): 945–55.

Pierce, Jessica. *The Last Walk.* Chicago: University of Chicago Press, 2012.

Pilkington, Ed. "'Paris Hilton Syndrome' Strikes California Animal Shelters." *The Guardian,* December 10, 2009. Accessed November 6, 2021. https://www.theguardian.com/world/2009/dec/10/chihuahuas-paris-hilton-syndrome.

Ratcliff, Ace Tilton. "How Starting a Pet Euthanasia Business Saved My Life." *Narratively,* June 17, 2019. Accessed July 30, 2019. https://narratively.com/how-starting-a-pet-euthanasia-business-saved-my-life/.

Sabin, Dyani. "A Pet's Death Can Hurt More Than Losing a Fellow Human." *Popular Science,* May 1, 2018. Accessed July 26, 2019. https://www.popsci.com/pet-death-grief/.

Shaw, Jane R., and Laurel Lagoni. "End-of-Life Communication in Veterinary Medicine: Delivering Bad News and Euthanasia Decision Making." *Veterinary Clinics: Small Animal Practice* 37 (2007): 95–108.

Thayer, Kate. "Veterinarians Work to Prevent Suicide as Study Finds Increased Risk: 'There Is Absolutely Nothing Weak About Asking for Help.'" *Chicago Tribune,* January 28, 2019. Accessed April 29, 2019. https://www.chicagotribune.com/lifestyles/ct-life-veterinarians-suicide-20190108-story.html.

Tomasi, Suzanne E., Ethan D. Fechter-Leggett, Nicole T. Edwards, Anna D. Reddish, Alex E. Crosby, and Randall J. Nett. "Suicide Among Veterinarians in the United States from 1979 through 2015." *Journal of the American Veterinary Medical Association* 254, no. 1 (January 1, 2019): 104–12.

CHAPTER 4: TURTLES & TAXIDERMY

Boboltz, Sara. "That Crazy Tortoise Story on 'Transparent' Actually Happened." *Huffpost,* September 26, 2016. Accessed June 3, 2019. https://www.huffpost.com/entry/that-crazy-tortoise-story-on-transparent-actually-happened_n_57e953bae4b08d73b83281c1.

Boss, Pauline. *Ambiguous Loss: Learning to Live with Unresolved Grief.* Cambridge, MA: Harvard University Press, 1999.

Carroll, Stephanie. "Why Were Victorians Obsessed with Death?" *Unhinged Historian* (blog), November 7, 2012. Accessed June 3, 2019. http://www.unhingedhistorian.com/2012/11/why-were-victorians-obsessed-with-death.html?q=obsessed+with+death.

"Charles Dickens' Letter Opener." 1862. Henry W. and Albert A. Berg Collection of English and American Literature. New York Public Library Digital Collections. Accessed October 18, 2021. https://digitalcollections.nypl.org/items/52ebd640-93d6-0134-0164-00505686a51c.

Horn, Leslie. "Charles Dickens Turned His Dead Cat's Paw into a Letter Opener." *Gizmodo,* December 19, 2012. Accessed February 22, 2018. https://gizmodo.com/5969719/charles-dickens-turned-his-dead-cats-paw-into-a-letter-opener.

"It All Started with a Dead Cat Drone—Now Is a Taxidermy Drone Company." *Dronethusiast.* Accessed October 17, 2021. https://www.dronethusiast.com/dead-cat-drone/.

Marbury, Robert. *Taxidermy Art: A Rogue's Guide to the Work, the Culture, and How to Do It Yourself.* New York: Artisan, 2014.

Maynard, Jake. "Freeze-Dried Pets Are Forever." *Slate,* November 14, 2019. Accessed December 6, 2019. https://slate.com /technology/2019/11/why-people-freeze-dry-their-pets-and -how-it-happens.html.

Messenger, Stephen. "Family Cleans House, Finds Pet Tortoise Missing Since 1982." *Treehugger,* February 4, 2013. Accessed June 3, 2019. https://www.treehugger.com/natural-sciences /family-cleans-house-and-finds-pet-tortoise-went-missing-30 -years-earlier.html.

Morris, Pat, with Joanna Ebenstein. *Walter Potter's Curious World of Taxidermy.* New York: Blue Rider, 2014.

Perkins, Anne. "How to Dispose of a Dead Pet: Is Taxidermy the Very Best Option?" *The Guardian,* December 4, 2017. Accessed July 17, 2019. https://www.theguardian.com/life andstyle/2017/dec/04/how-to-dispose-of-a-dead-pet-is-taxi dermy-the-very-best-option.

Turner, Alexis. *Taxidermy.* New York: Rizzoli International, 2013.

Wee, Sui-Lee. "His Cat's Death Left Him Heartbroken, So He Cloned It." *New York Times,* September 4, 2019. Accessed December 6, 2019. https://www.nytimes.com/2019/09/04 /business/china-cat-clone.html.

CHAPTER 5: BETTAS & BURIALS

Ambros, Barbara. *Bones of Contention: Animals and Religion in Contemporary Japan.* Honolulu: University of Hawai'i Press, 2012.

Ancient Nubia Now. Exhibition, October 13, 2019–January 20, 2020. Museum of Fine Arts, Boston. https://www.mfa.org /exhibitions/nubia.

Bischoff, Paul. "China Dog Lovers Pay Thousands for Luxury Pet Funerals." *Mashable,* September 4, 2015. Accessed June 24, 2019. https://mashable.com/2015/09/04/pet-funerals-china/.

Browne, Sylvia. *All Pets Go to Heaven.* New York: Atria, 2009.

Chalfen, Richard. "Celebrating Life After Death: The Appearance of Snapshots in Japanese Pet Gravesites." *Visual Studies* 18, no. 2 (2003): 144–56.

Deutsch, Otto Erich. *Mozart: A Documentary Biography.* Stanford, CA: Stanford University Press, 1965.

Doughty, Caitlin (@thegooddeath). "'In Memory of Little Joe. Died November 3rd 1875. Aged 3 Years' Little Joe was a canary y'all! This taxidermy piece is from 19th century England." Instagram, June 30, 2017. Accessed March 20, 2019. https://www.instagram.com/p/BV-yQtfDIhI/?hl=en&taken -by=thegooddeath.

Gilman, Clarabel. "Some Animals of the Northern Hemisphere." *Journal of Education* 60, no. 14 (October 6, 1904): 233–34.

Haupt, Lyanda Lynn. *Mozart's Starling.* New York: Little, Brown, 2017.

Hobgood-Oster, Laura. *Holy Dogs and Asses: Animals in the Christian Tradition.* Chicago: University of Illinois Press, 2008.

Huang, Echo. "Pet Owners in China Are Splurging on Luxury Hotels, Acupuncture Treatments, and Fancy Funerals." *Quartz,* August 29, 2017. Accessed June 24, 2019. https://qz .com/1064439/pet-owners-in-china-are-splurging-on-luxury -hotels-acupuncture-treatments-and-fancy-funerals/.

Hung, Louise. "Mourning Mosa: My Cat's Funeral in Japan." Order of the Good Death (website). March 5, 2017. Accessed June 28, 2019. https://www.orderofthegooddeath.com /article/mourning-mosa-my-cats-funeral-in-japan/.

Kenney, Elizabeth. "Pet Funerals and Animal Graves in Japan." *Mortality* 9, no. 1 (February 2004): 42–60.

Metcalfe, Tom. "2,000-Year-Old Dog Graveyard Discovered in Siberia." *Live Science,* July 15, 2016. Accessed April 18, 2018. https://www.livescience.com/55415-ancient-dog-graveyard -discovered.html.

mike_pants. "A Victorian sarcophagus, brass and marble. Inside is a shrouded bluebird with this note: 'Our pet Wee-Wee, Died Monday 18 June, 1874 at 7:55 o'clock.'" ArtefactPorn. Reddit. March 4, 2015. Accessed March 20, 2019. https://www.reddit.com/r/ArtefactPorn/comments/2xws2p/a _victorian_sarcophagus_brass_and_marble_inside/.

Niemetschek, Franz. *Life of Mozart.* Translated by Helen Mautner. London: Leonard Hyman, 1956. Originally written in 1798.

Pennisi, Elizabeth. "Burials in Cyprus Suggest Cats Were Ancient Pets." *Science* 304, no. 5668 (April 9, 2004): 189.

Rohr, Richard. *The Universal Christ: How a Forgotten Reality Can Change Everything We See, Hope For, and Believe.* New York: Convergent Books, 2019.

Sife, Wallace. *The Loss of a Pet.* 3rd ed. Hoboken, NJ: Howell Book House, 2005.

Veldkamp, Elmer. "The Emergence of 'Pets as Family' and the Socio-Historical Development of Pet Funerals in Japan." *Anthrozoös* 22, no. 4 (2009): 333–46.

Wapnish, Paula, and Brian Hesse. "Pampered Pooches or Plain Pariahs? The Ashkelon Dog Burials." *Biblical Archaeologist* 56, no. 2 (June 1993): 50–80.

West, Meredith J., and Andrew P. King. "Mozart's Starling." *American Scientist* 78 (March–April 1990): 106–14.

CHAPTER 6: STALLIONS & STARDOM

Bouyea, Brien, ed. *National Museum of Racing and Hall of Fame Official Guide 2017–2018.* Saratoga Springs, NY: National Museum of Racing and Hall of Fame.

Crist, Steven. "Secretariat, Racing Legend and Fans' Favorite, Is Dead." *New York Times,* October 5, 1989. Accessed September 5, 2019. https://www.nytimes.com/1989/10/05/sports /secretariat-racing-legend-and-fans-favorite-is-dead.html.

Gilliland, Haley Cohen. "Why Explosives Detectors Still Can't Beat a Dog's Nose." *MIT Technology Review,* October 24, 2019. Accessed January 31, 2020. https://www.technologyreview .com/2019/10/24/132201/explosives-detectors-dogs-nose -sensors/.

Livingston, Barbara. "Man o' War's Funeral: Remarkable Final Tribute for a Majestic Champion." *Daily Racing Form,* February 24, 2011. Accessed September 5, 2019. https://www .drf.com/blogs/man-o-wars-funeral-remarkable-final-tribute -majestic-champion.

Mull, Amanda. "The Inevitable Aging of the Internet's Famous Pets." *The Atlantic,* January 28, 2019. Accessed September 26, 2019. https://www.theatlantic.com/health/archive/2019 /01/pet-communities-are-last-nice-place-online/581440/.

Ohlheiser, Abby. "This Decade Taught Us to Love Viral Pets. Now We Have to Grieve Their Deaths." *Washington Post,* December 2, 2019. Accessed January 23, 2020. https://www.washingtonpost.com/technology/2019/12/02/this-decade-taught-us-love-viral-pets-now-we-have-grieve-their-deaths/.

Santiago, Amanda Luz Henning. "What Happens When an Animal Influencer Dies?" *Mashable,* August 8, 2018. Accessed September 27, 2019. mashable.com/article/when-animal-influencers-die/.

CHAPTER 7: FELINES & FEELINGS

Bekoff, Marc. *Strolling with Our Kin: Speaking for and Respecting Voiceless Animals.* New York: Lantern/Booklight, 2000.

Berg, Matt. "Ms. Jennifer, 53-Year-Old Tortoise, Up for Adoption After Owner Dies of COVID-19." *Boston Globe,* May 21, 2020. Accessed November 6, 2021. https://www.bostonglobe.com/2020/05/21/metro/ms-jennifer-53-year-old-tortoise-up-adoption-after-owner-died-covid-19/.

Cuthbert, Lori, and Douglas Main. "Orca Mother Drops Calf, After Unprecedented 17 Days of Mourning." *National Geographic,* August 13, 2018. Accessed November 6, 2021. https://www.nationalgeographic.com/animals/2018/08/orca-mourning-calf-killer-whale-northwest-news/.

"The Dog Suicide Bridge." Atlas Obscura Community. *Atlas Obscura.* Accessed October 17, 2021. https://community.atlasobscura.com/t/the-dog-suicide-bridge/9136.

Dosa, David. *Making Rounds with Oscar.* New York: Hyperion, 2010.

Engelhaupt, Erika. "Would Your Dog Eat You If You Died? Get the Facts." *National Geographic,* June 23, 2017. Accessed January 22, 2020. https://www.nationalgeographic.com/news /2017/06/pets-dogs-cats-eat-dead-owners-forensics-science.

Kindon, Frances, and Vicki Newman. "Michael Jackson's Chimp Bubbles 'Tried to Commit Suicide, Was Beaten and Self-Harmed.'" *The Mirror,* February 16, 2019. Accessed September 12, 2019. https://www.mirror.co.uk/3am/celebrity-news /michael-jacksons-chimp-bubbles-tried-14007221.

King, Barbara J. *How Animals Grieve.* Chicago: University of Chicago Press, 2013.

Lemish, Michael. *War Dogs.* Sterling, VA: Brassey's, 1999.

Malki, Jason. "Author Dr. Christopher Kerr: Dying Needs to Be Recognized as More Than Medical Failure or the Physical Suffering We Either Observe or Experience." *Authority Magazine,* July 29, 2020. Accessed January 4, 2022.

Masson, Jeffrey Moussaieff. *Dogs Never Lie About Love: Reflections on the Emotional World of Dogs.* New York: Crown, 1997.

McDonnell, Sharon. "Memorable Mutts: 11 Dogs Monuments Around the World." *Fodor's Travel,* September 18, 2017. Accessed March 25, 2019. https://www.fodors.com/news /photos/memorable-mutts-11-dogs-monuments-around-the -world.

McGraw, Carol. "Gorilla's Pet: Koko Mourns Kitten's Death." *Los Angeles Times,* January 10, 1985. Accessed September 13, 2019. https://www.latimes.com/archives/la-xpm-1985-01-10 -mn-9038-story.html.

Nir, Sarah Maslin. "The Pets Left Behind by Covid-19." *New York Times,* June 23, 2020. Accessed November 6, 2021.

https://www.nytimes.com/2020/06/23/nyregion/coronavirus
-pets.html.

Nunez, Sigrid. *The Friend.* New York: Penguin Random House,
2018.

———. *Mitz: The Marmoset of Bloomsbury.* New York: Soft
Skull, 2019.

Riley, Christopher. "The Dolphin Who Loved Me: The NASA-
Funded Project That Went Wrong." *The Guardian,* June 8,
2014. Accessed 22 January 2020. https://www.theguardian
.com/environment/2014/jun/08/the-dolphin-who-loved-me.

Safina, Carl. "The Depths of Animal Grief." Nova (website).
Article published July 8, 2015. Accessed November 6, 2021.
https://www.pbs.org/wgbh/nova/article/animal-grief/.

Scannell, Kara. "This Is What Happens to the Pets Left Behind
When Their Owners Die from Coronavirus." CNN, May
12, 2020. Accessed November 6, 2021. https://www.cnn.com
/2020/05/12/us/pets-of-coronavirus/index.html.

Siebert, Charles. "An Elephant Crackup?" *New York Times,* October 8, 2006. Accessed November 6, 2021. https://www
.nytimes.com/2006/10/08/magazine/08elephant.html.

"We've Bred Dogs to Have Expressive Eyebrows That Manipulate Our Emotions." *CBC Radio,* June 21, 2019. Accessed
November 6, 2021. https://www.cbc.ca/radio/quirks/june-22
-is-your-wi-fi-watching-you-dog-s-manipulative-eyebrows
-darwin-s-finches-in-danger-and-more-1.5182752/we-ve-bred
-dogs-to-have-expressive-eyebrows-that-manipulate-our
-emotions-1.5182767.

Yeginsu, Ceylan. "'Dog Suicide Bridge': Why Do So Many
Pets Keep Leaping Into a Scottish Gorge?" *New York Times,*

March 27, 2019. Accessed April 4, 2019. https://www.nytimes .com/2019/03/27/world/europe/scotland-overtoun-bridge -dog-suicide.html.

CHAPTER 8: CANINES & COMMUNITY

Beck, Julie. "How Dogs Make Friends for Their Humans." *The Atlantic,* November 30, 2015. Accessed January 21, 2020. https://www.theatlantic.com/health/archive/2015/11/how -dogs-make-friends-for-their-humans/417645/.

Gevinson, Tavi, ed. *Rookie on Love: 45 Voices on Romance, Friend-ship, and Self-Care.* New York: Razorbill, 2018.

O'Neill, Eugene. *The Last Will and Testament of an Extremely Distinguished Dog.* Carlisle, MA: Applewood Books, 2014.

EPILOGUE

Mogolov, Lisa Scanlon. "The Heart of a Pet." *Wellesley,* Summer 2018. Accessed November 6, 2021. https://magazine.wellesley .edu/summer-2018/the-heart-pet.

Weiner, Eric. "Bhutan's Dark Secret to Happiness." *BBC Travel,* April 8, 2015. Accessed November 6, 2021. https://www .bbc.com/travel/article/20150408-bhutans-dark-secret-to -happiness.

Acknowledgments

First and foremost, thank you to every single person I interviewed for this book, especially those of you who shared deeply personal and hard stories about the deaths of your pets. Your enthusiasm for this project, your excitement that a book like this would exist, and your willingness to talk about some extremely painful memories for the sake of my research — for that I am eternally indebted. This book would not exist without you. In particular, thank you to: Midori Allen, Shelly Anand, Nina Bargiel, Ben Braithwaite-Vaquerano, Mitch Byers, Yoshi Campbell, Tim Carey, Douglas Clark, Molly Colvin, Michael D'Aresta and the entire Middletown Police Department, Sabrina D'Souza, Angela Daniels-Valenzuela, Meredith Davis-Yelinek, Hadley Dion, Jeanne Dooley, Joyce Eldridge, Larry Eldridge, Jill Gallagher, Alex Gardiner, Francis Giles, Elizabeth Jane Good, Annie Hartnett, Erin

Hilley, Caroline Holland, Samantha Irby, Andrew Johnson, Kate Katulak, Kea Krause, Shweta Ganesh Kumar, Monica La Vita, Heather Magers, Eleanor Miller, Sy Montgomery, Mariel Novas, Vern Pena, Kate Putnam, Tucker Rosebrock, Abbigail N. Rosewood, Donna Ross, Adam Ruben, Amy Sawan, Nina Silva, Cassie J. Sneider, Hannah Sokol, Laura Jane Standley, Will Stegemann, Jill Walsh, Artress Bethany White, Aarin Wright, Jaime Zuckerman, and John and his cloned pups. Thank you to every person who, even in passing, when hearing what I was working on, wanted to tell me about their own dead pets. I love nothing more than hearing about the animals that you all have loved. I am sorry I was not able to fit every one of your stories into these pages, but know that each of them helped my thinking and understanding for this book in so many ways. I could not have done it without you all. Thank you.

In addition to the pet owners, thank you to all the animal professionals I spoke with for this project, many of whom shared with me their own stories of love and loss as well: Divya Anantharaman, Gail Arnold, Marie Beavers, Dr. Philip Bergman, Eliza Blanchard, Jennifer Breslow, Bishop Thomas Brown, Dr. Derek Calhoon, Dr. Stephen Carr, Dr. Alli Coates, Susan P. Cohen, Merry Coor, Sandy Darling, Dillon Eaves, Michael Elliot, Dr. Sandi Farris, Kerry O. Furlani, Eric Greene, Christine Hansen,

Heide Hatry, Ed Hildebrandt, Leon Hill, Salima Ikram, Lauren Kane-Lysak, Cheri Keches, Thea Keith-Lucas, Dr. Bennett King, Doug Korn, Codi Lamb, Isa Leshko, Paul Manganaro, Dr. Indu Mani, Ed Martin Jr., Dr. Terri McGinnis, Dr. Dani McVety, Dia Moeller, Bill Morgan, Dr. Katie Moynihan, Mary Peng, Dr. Lisa Radosta, Ace Tilton Ratcliff, Dr. Yvonne Schulman, Nick Sinclair, Wendy Van de Poll, Paul M. Vanecko, Fran Weil, Simone Pixley Weinstein, Dr. Marilyn Welsh, John White, Jennifer Williams, and Mike at Pet's Rest Cemetery, in Colma, California, whose last name I never got, plus many, many more. I am also deeply grateful to every person who connected me to one of these knowledgeable individuals—so many friends of friends of friends made this book possible.

Thank you to every single person who sent me articles, stories, photos, videos, memes—really, anything and everything relevant to dead pets (or alive pets!) out there on the internet. I feel like I had hundreds of research assistants in writing this book. New friends, old friends, family, extended family, future family, former classmates, former students, current students, classmates from middle school and high school and college, neighbors, acquaintances—so many people came out of the woodwork to help me with this book. Thank you! It made me so happy every time I would get a message on Instagram or Facebook or Twitter from someone I hadn't spoken to in a while but who wanted to reach out with a "Hey, in case you missed it . . ." note and a link to a turtle obituary or an article about a cloned cat. An enormous thank-you to my closest friends, who really became my core research team, doing everything from searching for dog mummies in Peru (Janna) to harassing the staff of London's Hyde Park Pet Cemetery (Melissa) to translating Spanish pet headstones in Miami (Meri) to hunting down every Japanese pet funeral expert (Lee) to hunting for ghost cats in Concord (Tuck and Liz) to connecting me to all the pet care professionals in China (Ami Li) to sending me ARCs of every pet and animal book (Nikki) to giving me private tours of secret Wayland pet cemeteries (Laura Yams) to taking photos of pet graves all over Maine (Hayley, Jon, and Malina) to being my unofficial legal counsel (Erin B.) to literally living with me through this (Erin G.). I also owe the Wellesley Wags and Whiskers Facebook group big-time for always coming through when I needed to crowdsource an idea or question. Thank you also to the horse-racing subreddit (r/horseracing) for helping me find the answer to my most obscure research question.

Thank you to the many readers and editors who have been with this project since the beginning, especially Laura Jane Standley, Kea Krause, Elisabeth Sherman, Nick Lehr, Ariel Hubbard, Mary Mann, Deborah Cannarella, Bri Fasone, Sebastian Deken, and my very first workshop group at Columbia ("the Wolf Pack"), who helped me shape those early dead-pet tales ("tails"). An enormous thank-you to Nina MacLaughlin, whose eyes lit up when I first mentioned this book idea, who encouraged me to pursue it, and who helped make it a reality. Thank you to Kelly J. Ford, Elizabeth Chiles Shelburne, Michele Ferrari, and Rachel Barenbaum for those Thursday pump-up sessions at Shays. Thank you to Frankie Moisin, Lauren Scovel, Michelle Kuo, Kelly Ramsey, and Jaime Zuckerman, who also all read early versions of this book and provided thoughtful insights and helpful feedback. Sorry you had to slog through those terrible first drafts, but the book would not be what it is without you.

Thank you to all of the places that generously published early versions or variations of the stories that appear in this book, including *The Millions, xoJane, Thimble Literary Magazine,* and *Wellesley.* (Speaking of Wellesley, thank you to Lisa Scanlon Mogolov for having a picnic with me at the grave of Katherine Lee Bates's collie, Sigurd.) A special thank-you to Nicole Cliffe, who ran a three-part series of my stories called "Dead Pet Chronicles" on *The Toast* in 2014.

Thank you to the Cambridge Public Library for being my office and number one research center. I spent time in every one of your branches working on this book, though the main branch will always hold a special place in my heart. (So many not-dead dogs to watch on the lawn out-side!) Thank you also to the Boston Public Library, the New York Public Library, the Fishers Island Library, and all the libraries in the Minuteman Library Network, espe-cially Robbins Library, in Arlington. Also, libraries would not be what they are without librarians — thank you to all those who dug up interlibrary loan items and requested out-of-print dead-pet picture books on my behalf, but also thank you to all the librarians who, along the way, helped shape the writer and reader I am today. In particular, thank you to Susannah Borysthen-Tkacz, Talya Sokoll, Emily Tragert, Adele Cooper, Gail Harris, Masha Kantarovsky, and Ann Banks.

Thank you to the Catwalk Institute for giving me the time and space to write and research nonstop for the better part of September 2018, and thank you to the places that have employed me throughout the writing of this book that have also granted me time and space. GrubStreet al-lowed me to have a malleable schedule and didn't mind if I disappeared for a month to go to a residency. The No-ble and Greenough School not only didn't mind when I quit teaching full-time to write but actively encouraged it, and I'm grateful to the Wellesley College Communications and Public Affairs team for being flexible, accommodat-ing, and, possibly, even more excited about this book than I am. It's a dream to work with you! And, of course, a special shout-out to Newtonville Books for its ongoing support and encouragement—I knew you would be from the day of my interview, when Mary Cotton and I bonded over our dead pets. (Thanks in advance for the kick-ass launch party!)

In addition to Newtonville, thank you to so many independent bookstores—you help me track down books, you host inspiring author events, you foster literary community, you make me feel comfortable and at home, and you make the world a better place. In particular: Porter Square Books, Harvard Book Store, Belmont Books, Brookline Booksmith, Wellesley Books, Book Ends, Papercuts J.P., The Silver Unicorn Bookstore, Eight Cousins, McNally Jackson, Books Are Magic, and Greenlight Bookstore.

Thank you to all my students—from GrubStreet, from Nobles, from Mother Caroline, from everywhere—for your enthusiasm and encouragement. It can be really hard to keep up momentum writing a book, and one thing that kept me going was knowing I had promised to you all that I was going to do this thing. So here it is. And hey, Nobles class of 2020, remember when I said you all would be in college by the time this book came out? I was right.

Thank you to all my teachers—from Lexington Montessori, from Nashoba Brooks, from Nobles, from Wellesley, from Columbia—for making me a writer and a reader. You noticed what I was good at, you encouraged me to keep at it, you pushed me to do better. I would not be a writer today without your support. In particular, thank you to Sue Wurster, Nina Freeman, Sarah Dickenson Snyder, Vicky Seelen, Julia Russell, Kate Coon, Peter Raymond, Tim Carey, Marilyn Sides, Thomas Hodge, Alla Epsteyn, Adam Weiner, Lis Harris, Phillip Lopate, Cris Beam, Margo Jefferson, Patricia O'Toole, and Ben Taylor. Thank you also to Barbara Gray, who has taught me a lot about myself in the past ten years.

Thank you to every person who has ever read, promoted, and/or encouraged my work. You keep me going. To my book club, People Who Read Darkness — you are the most enthusiastic readers and my target demographic! Thank you to all of you who subscribe to and read my newsletter, who repost things that I write, who come to my events, who make me feel like what I am doing is actually worthwhile. Thank you to Sarah Pruski, who made my glorious website! You made something so gorgeous, I want to be a better writer to live up to the hype. You are such a cheerleader of my work — thank you.

Speaking of cheerleaders, thank you to my agent extraordinaire, Gillian MacKenzie, for immediately understanding this project and sending me articles about Barbra Streisand's cloned dogs and the dead hamster on Spirit Airlines before you were even officially representing me. From the minute we met, I knew you were the right agent for me. Thank you to the entire team at Gillian MacKenzie Agency, plus all the lovely people at the Marsh Agency and Wolf Literary Services for their support and encouragement. I feel so lucky to be part of this gang.

Speaking of feeling lucky, most books only get one editor—this book got to have two, and both are extraordinary. The most immense thank-you to the kind and thoughtful genius Naomi Gibbs for first championing this book, for helping me figure out the story I wanted to tell, and for always liking all of my #deadpets content on Twitter and Instagram. Thank you for putting up with me overwriting and over-quoting and gently but firmly guiding me back to my main questions and helping me cut down to the core of what I was trying to get at. You regularly seemed to understand what I was trying to say before I knew what I was trying to say. It was, quite literally, a dream come true to work with you! And all the overwhelming gratitude to the great and fearless Ivy Givens, who picked up where Naomi left off, shepherding this book into its final form. I knew you were the perfect editor for this book as soon as you told me about your horses and turtles. You get it, and you have been enthusiastically cheering this book on from behind the scenes since long before you officially took over! You are the best! Thank you!

And, of course, thank you to the whole team at Mariner Books (née Houghton Mifflin Harcourt Books & Media) and HarperCollins—what would I do without you all? In particular, thank you to Jenny Xu, Francesca Carlos, Hannah Dirgins, Lisa Glover, Laura Brady, and Chloe Foster. Thank you to Will Palmer, copy editor extraordinaire, and proofreader Rachael DeShano! Thank you to the extremely patient Mark Robinson for the beautiful cover, to Emily Snyder for the gorgeous interior design, and to Anna Llorens, who brought so many of my pets back from the dead with her gorgeous illustrations. And a special thank-you to Bruce Nichols, for the perfect subtitle.

And, naturally, the biggest thank-you of all to my family, who both tolerated and encouraged my obsession with pets for the past thirty-four years. Thank you to my grandparents, Nunni and Puppy, who always took care of my childhood birds and dogs when we were out of town, who finally gave up on trying to convince me to be a doctor or a lawyer and then went full force encouraging this whole writing business, who proudly brag to all of their friends and hairdressers and doctors that their granddaughter is writing a book. Nunni and Puppy also provided financial support in grad school and beyond, and I would not have been able to write as much as I have the past ten years without their help. Thank you. I am so lucky to be your granddaughter.

Thank you to my siblings, Chad, Sara, and Gen, and my sister-in-law, Becca, who helped me rescue turtles from the middle of the road and taught Gus and Gwen to jump up on the sofa. Thank you to my niece, Agnes, and my nephews, Graham and Bobby, for sharing my love of animals and being down to chat about reptiles. You three are the most gentle, compassionate, and empathetic to creatures of all species, and I admire you for it.

Thank you to Kristine, Rich, and Kailyn for always asking about my book and checking in on Terrence — I knew I had found the right family to marry into when I first walked into your home and saw Cocoa's ashes displayed on the bookshelf. A special shout-out to Connie and a promise that I will get a large-print version of this book just for you. And thank you to the entire extended Doyle-Nee-Corrado family — you have welcomed me into your tribe and shared your pet stories with me, and it feels so good to know that all of you have my back. Thank you.

There are several people who did not live to see the publication of this book. While I so wish they were able to see this book in person, I have felt their love and support throughout the whole process: Charles Richard Bartels Sr. ("Papa B"), Christine Andersen McHugh, Gene Bartels Wichmann, Dori Davis, William H. Kehlenbeck, and Donna Casper.

An impossibly large thank-you to my parents: to my mom, Karen, for allowing all these creatures into her fastidious home in the first place, and to my dad, Rich, who was always my number one ally in obtaining pets. You two have provided me with love, encouragement, and all types of support—from emotional to promotional to financial and everything in between—my entire life, and I would not have been able to write this book, would not be a writer at all, without you two. I don't know what else to say but thank you, thank you, thank you, thank you, thank you, thank you.

Thank you to all the pets—dead and alive—who enriched my life in so many ways: your unconditional love and the joy you brought me is what makes life worth living. A special thank-you to Seymour, Terrence ("Mr. T"), Bert, Lieutenant Dan, and the Miltons. Thank you also to all the pets I met through this book—dead and alive —who have shared their lives with others. Hearing about your personalities, your quirks, the ways you brought your people joy . . . well, I mean, that is what this book is all about.

And finally, my greatest gratitude goes to my husband, Richie, for always standing by me, even if at times it was difficult to share a home with so many depressing dead-pet research materials. Thank you for always believing in me, for giving me pep talks when I felt like there was no way I could actually write an entire book, for encouraging me to quit jobs and pursue dreams, for being even more fiercely protective of my writing time than I am, for cooking me a whole bunch of food, for holding down a steady job while I attempted to freelance, for keeping our pets alive while I was traveling for research or residencies, and for always being down for a trip to Petco. You love animals so much that just seeing the cover of *When a Pet Dies,* by Fred Rogers, makes you cry, and that's why I love you. You get it. Thank you.